THIS WILL BE THE LAST TIME
LOUISE RYAN

THIS WILL BE THE LAST TIME

LOUISE RYAN

Copyright © Louise Ryan 2024

Published by Joanne Fedler Media 2024
www.joannefedler.com

The author and Joanne Fedler Media acknowledge and honour that this book was published on the land of the First Nations people of Australia. We pay our respects to their Elders past and present.

Hardcover
ISBN: 978-1-925842-57-9

Paperback
ISBN: 978-1-925842-53-1

Ebook
ISBN: 978-1-925842-54-8

Audiobook:
ISBN: 978-1-925842-55-5

Cover Design by
Bahrina Kasih

Typesetting by Brandon Daniel
www.viewpointstudio.co.uk

All rights reserved. The author asserts her moral rights in this work through the world without waiver. No part of this book may be reproduced, or stored in a retrieval system, or transmitted in any form or by any means, electronic, mechanical, photocopying, recording or otherwise without express written permission of the publisher.

DEDICATION

*To my younger self:
to the child who never was;
and to all those whose
childhoods were lost.*

TABLE OF CONTENTS

ACT 1	1	CROSSING THE THRESHOLD	11
THE VISIT	2	THE LETTER (PART 1)	16
	3	FLYING HIGH	21
	4	MEDICAL MATTERS	30
	5	ACTING THE PART	38
	6	MUSICAL INTERLUDES	46
	7	KISS ME GOODNIGHT, SERGEANT MAJOR	51
	8	GOING TO THE MOVIES	58
ACT 2	9	THE DARKNESS	65
FLASHBACK	10	MOVING TO AUSTRALIA	71
	11	THE CHAIR	79
	12	THE DRESSING GOWN	83
	13	THE KARATE KID	88
	14	THE TORCH	93
	15	LEAVING HOME	97
	16	THE CONVERSATION	101
ACT 3	17	THE UNRAVELLING	109
FLASHFORWARD	18	SECRET NO MORE	118
	19	A WOMAN AMONG MEN	133
	20	AN EXPAT EXPERIENCE	140
	21	COMING HOME	151
	22	THE DIAGNOSIS	155
	23	THE TREATMENTS	162
	24	THE AFTERMATH	171
	25	MORE QUESTIONS THAN ANSWERS	174
	26	A SIZEABLE PROBLEM	177
	27	THE LOST CHILD	183
ACT 4	28	A NEW COURAGE	189
THE FINAL	29	THE LETTER (PART 2)	202
CURTAIN	30	EXIT, STAGE RIGHT	205
		POSTSCRIPT	211
		ACKNOWLEDGEMENTS	216
		ABOUT THE AUTHOR	218

ACT 1
THE VISIT

CROSSING THE THRESHOLD

August 2016
If I had been asked to pick him out of a police line-up, I could not have done it. His tiny 96-year-old frame was smothered under the institutionalised blanket, and the smell of antiseptic was overwhelming. I clutched the wad of tissues, and from the back of my parched throat, I finally managed, 'Hello, Dad.'

These words seemed so normal and yet, for the past eighteen years, I had not imagined that I would ever utter them again. Only moments before, I'd made my first tentative steps into this building—steps I swore I would never take.

'Can I help you?' The woman wore a tight-fitting tunic over navy trousers, her feet shod in clearly comfortable shoes. From the weary, welcoming smile, it was evident that she was used to meeting uncertain, anxious visitors who poked their heads through the doors of this purgatorial waiting room.

I told her the name of the person I had come to see.
'Come with me and I'll show you to his room.'

I had followed her through the lounge, where several residents were asleep in front of a large-screen TV, its increased decibels insufficient to disturb their slumber. I had imagined this path well before my arrival—I would walk down a passageway, turn left and his room would be the fourth on the right.

I was close—astonishingly. Down the passageway, turn left and it was the third room on the right. So far, no surprises. A perfectly normal, predictable outing.

I had flown in from Brisbane to make this visit. Others had offered to come with me, for 'moral support,' but this was to be a lone pilgrimage, a trek along a Camino trail of my own making. And I was now reaching my destination, my own version of Santiago de Compostela. During my travels, I had pondered the impending reunion, had played all possible scenarios over and over, and reminded myself that until that threshold had been crossed, the meeting could be delayed, deferred or even cancelled, with no consequences. But was that true? Would there be no consequences?

I had come—drawn by a force that seemed greater than myself, a force that knew the passage of time and was conscious of a life rising to its final crescendo, then falling to its inevitable diminuendo.

It was the receipt of a letter some months earlier that had set me on this path, that had led to the very door where I now found myself poised, waiting to cross that final chasm, like a long-jump champion who has just taken off and is soaring over the sand below. A sense of anticipation. A leap of faith.

As I peered into the room, I saw a series of shelves along one wall, which were laid out with great care— a modern-day reliquary, a microcosm of his life encapsulated in a handful of significant, historical objects, books and CDs. Each item had been carefully chosen and deliberately placed, displayed to best advantage. Is this how we are all to be finally represented? A lifetime of memories and endeavours condensed on a bookshelf?

My two-word greeting was still unanswered, hovering in the stillness. The woman was leaning over his swaddled form. Her voice, while precise and firm, was kind. 'You have a visitor. Your daughter is here.' I had been announced—there was no turning back.

I moved from my place of safety and approached his wheeled, reclining chair.

His face so small, his hollow cheeks covered in skin that was the colour and texture of ancient parchment, his eyes, still so blue, sitting in their now crinkled, sunken sockets, were searching my face, trying to focus, to remember.

'Hi, Dad.' The emotion of the occasion was now washing over me. I unfurled one of the tissues and wiped away the torrents of tears from my face and under my chin. 'It's Louise.'

He spoke, the struggle evident between his brain and his vocal cords.

'It is wonderful to see you.'

'It's good to see you too, Dad.' The sincerity and truth of these words took me by surprise.

'I can't believe it,' he said. 'I really can't believe it.' A tear fell from the corner of his eye and trickled down his cheek. I took another tissue and gently wiped the tear away, while I continued to sob.

He said, 'I am a bit confused. I wasn't expecting you until tomorrow.'

'Not until tomorrow?'

'No, not until Tuesday afternoon.'

'Dad, it *is* Tuesday afternoon.'

'Oh.' He looked bemused, then sad, as though he were disappointed in himself for no longer knowing the days of the week.

He was totally dependent on others for his care, unable to move without assistance. Surely, each day bore a remarkable similarity to the other.

'Would you have done anything differently if you had known that today was Tuesday?'

He managed a half-hearted shrug. 'I guess not,' he sighed, closing his eyes. He seemed to keep them shut for a long time, and it took me a while to realise that he had fallen asleep. I stared into his face, his mouth agape, his skeletal features unmistakeable in his haggard cheekbones, his hair still sufficient to cover his now tiny skull. I took his hand in mine and felt the bones of his fingers, so evident in his diminished state. He was so frail, so vulnerable, so helpless.

He seemed to sleep for a long time, but in reality, it was only a few moments. His eyes opened, refocused, and looked deep into my own.

We stared at each other in silence. I had imagined this moment for so long, imagined what I would say, had rehearsed the words in my head on so many occasions; but now that we were together, the words would not come.

ACT 1 — CROSSING THE THRESHOLD

He broke the silence.
'You look good,' he said. 'You still have great teeth. You always had great teeth.'
I felt my eyes lowering, self-conscious at his compliment. I was surprised that his approval still meant so much to me.
'Not bad for a fifty-seven-year-old, eh?'
He smiled, and then I truly recognised him. There was something so distinctive about his smile, familiar, yet haunting. It reminded me of times long past—the good times as well as the bad. It reflected his very essence, and I found myself transported back through the decades.

'Sshh—the fairies.'
Immediate silence, the bodies in the car breathed shallow so as not to disturb the unseen. It was an established family tradition, its origins long forgotten. Wherever, whenever the trees overhead would touch, blotting out the sun and sky, this hushed but urgent cry would emanate; and conversation would cease until the trees no longer met and the fairies, obviously, had vanished.
It had been a time of family, the familiar, well-known and well-loved practices, unaltered, predictable, safe and playful, for adults and children alike. A bonding ritual that lifted us, together, to a magical place where ethereal winged creatures lived an idyllic existence.
And for a few precious moments, so did we.

THE LETTER (PART 1)

October 2015
My father wrote me a letter that should never have needed to be written, or received; but when it arrived, I oddly, and surprisingly greatly anticipated it.

He did not know my address. I had severed all communication eighteen years earlier. Other family members had helped maintain this total blackout—no information was to be provided to him of my life, my successes or failures, my good health or otherwise. It was as though I had ceased to exist for him, and that had been my heartfelt intent.

The letter had been sent through my brother-in-law. He had enclosed the small white envelope in a larger package. He knew that receiving such a letter would cause untold and unknown emotions for me and he had enclosed a letter of his own, to soften the shock. He wrote, 'It is completely up to you whether to open or discard it.'

I knew that this day would come, that a letter would arrive. I had convinced myself that its delivery would affirm his death, his farewell testimony from the hereafter. In my mind, I had prepared a script that I needed him to follow—line by line, word by word. Anything less would be unacceptable.

I had not reckoned on receiving a letter in his lifetime. But discarding it was not an option.

For long days and nights, the letter had rested, unopened, on the kitchen bench of my pristine all-white Canberra apartment, with its modern furniture and its pleasant view overlooking the local cricket pitch.

He would have enjoyed the sight of the young Indian players who practised each evening in the cricket nets on the far side of the field, vying to be the next Sunil Gavaskar or Sachin Tendulkar. Many years ago, cricket had been one of our common interests. I had learned to score my brothers' matches, using the intricate symbols which represented the flow of the game—balls and no-balls, runs and overs. I used a sharpened HB pencil for this precise art form, where the scoresheet at the end of the day was a piece of papyrus, covered in sport-specific hieroglyphics. My expertise as a scorer was a source of pride to us both.

One day, when I was about twelve, the team was short a player and with no alternatives, I was allowed to take a bat out to the crease and face a couple of balls. I managed to carve out a few strokes, enough to finish the end of the innings for the team. This was my first foray into male-dominated pursuits.

As the sun set that day on the cricket pitch and my memories, I wondered when I might be ready to discover the envelope's content, unleash this genie from its bottle. Once the stopper had been pulled, it could never be replaced.

Four days later, I was ready. The apartment seemed an inappropriate location for such an event—too small, too intimate. I would always associate the contents of the letter with where I opened it, and I didn't know if that was something that I could live with every day. I decided that a special setting was required for its opening and, in spite of my ambivalent religious upbringing, chose a Catholic church, a kilometre from home.

The spring shrubs were beginning to bloom, and the cherry blossoms formed a pink honour guard for me.

Early the following Sunday afternoon, I entered the side chapel and slid into the back pew. However, instead of finding a place of solitude, the service was in its final throes. The priest was prompting the congregation in prayer and their mumbled responses echoed through the vaulted ceilings.

Supplication seemed appropriate and I lowered myself to the kneeler at my feet.

As I opened the envelope, I saw a small piece of lined paper, neatly folded into quarters. Naturally, it would have been neatly folded.

The writing was so familiar—a little crooked, somewhat shaky, but that carefully crafted lettering—so distinctive. I was terrified and excited, full of fear and anticipation.

What did my father have to say, after all these years? As I read, I began to cry—big gulping sobs, stifled due to the congregation around. Such a personal moment with such a public airing.

But this sobbing session was mine. I had earned it, I owned it and I was going to take it. As I caught my tears in the tissues, the organist began to play, and the choir began to sing.

The hymn's tune was so recognisable—Jerusalem. *'And did those feet in ancient times, walk upon England's mountains green...'* I travelled back in time and memory to the country of my beginnings. We had left that land of long icy winters, of Sheffield's *dark satanic mills,* for a new start in the largely unknown great southern land. It was a brave decision, taken fifty years ago, when the world was still naïve: when the Beatles were all that parents had to fear, and the *daleks* of Dr Who were all children had to fear.

I read the note only once. I couldn't see through my tears, and I was worried I'd ruin the letter. I restowed it in its envelope.

I moved into the body of the edifice, feeling its safe, sacred and spiritual vibrations.

The congregation was filing out and the church was almost empty. Perhaps now I would get my alone time. I wanted to read the letter again, paying particular attention to each phrase and nuance.

But I was not alone. The church was refilling—a family moved in from the left of the altar, another family from the right. A nominee of each was carrying a baby dressed in flowing white robes. Adults wore smart suits and their best dresses—some wore hats. Small children were dressed in miniature versions of the same outfits. It was time for the weekly christenings.

'And was the holy Lamb of God, on England's pleasant pastures seen...'

How fitting. The symbol of birth, rebirth and new beginnings, in this place, on this most significant of occasions. Infants being baptised to welcome them into the faith and to free them from the original sin with which they were born. If only our subsequent sins could be so easily freed—or forgiven.

Finding a seat well away from the invading families, I reopened the envelope. If I had been the author of its contents, I'd have changed the language, used another tone and focused on different content. But for all its flaws, the letter had been written. Now it had found its way to me, and I had chosen to open it—all of these variables had come together, perhaps as some greater power had intended. This was indeed the right location.

William Blake's words filled my head, *'Bring me my Spear... Bring me my Chariot of fire.'* For Blake, this was a call to the people of England to create a heaven on earth. For me, I wondered if it was a call to arms, a call to action.

With the strains of that hymn still playing in my head, I left the cool shadows of the church and stepped into the sunlight. My thoughts were filled with these newly uncovered words—words I had been waiting a lifetime to read.

FLYING HIGH

He'd fallen asleep again. As he had absented himself from the conversation, I moved from beside him and examined the shelves more closely.

A model aeroplane. A perfect replica of a Halifax bomber. I turned the four propellers, conscious of their fragility. It was a reminder of his days as a war hero. From an early age, we children were acutely aware of our father's wartime story. It was an integral part of our family's heritage and his legacy.

He had enlisted in the Royal Air Force and began flying Tiger Moths in 1941, before travelling to the United States in 1942 to train and qualify on more advanced planes.

In 1943, he had been based in the south of England, flying the life-sized version of the Halifax I held in my hands. In order to give this plane a longer flying range, the front and upper gun turrets were removed, and additional fuel tanks were attached below the wings and fuselage. Their sole purpose was to tow Horsa gliders, with three red-beret pilots, from

Cornwall to North Africa. Their final destination was Tunisia, where the gliders were destined to be used in the ill-fated invasion of Sicily.

It was a nine-hour flight to French Morocco, during which the pilots needed to maintain a speed of hundred and twenty-five knots. If they flew any faster, the stress on the glider's wings could prove dangerous to its structure, which could cause it to break into pieces. Flying below hundred and twenty-five knots meant that the aircraft would be in danger of stalling, causing both plane and the glider it was towing to plunge to the earth.

And so, while it was always remarkable to me that my father was a wartime pilot, the most astonishing aspect of his story was not that he was a flyer—it was that he survived a plane crash, into the Mediterranean Sea.

In September 1943, at the age of twenty-three, he was flying from Tunisia to Gibraltar, on a return journey to England, when one of the two port engines began to fail. It was not long before the second port engine stopped and the order to 'prepare for ditching' was given. As the co-pilot wrestled with the controls, my father turned his back towards the front of the plane to assist another crew member. The plane hit the water and he was thrown through the windscreen. The injuries to his back and legs were horrendous and life-threatening.

Despite that, he had managed to swim a few metres, where he was helped into one of the dinghies by fellow crew members. He'd lain on the bottom of the inflatable boat, in a pool of his own blood, wondering what fate awaited him. Within a few hours, a mast was sighted in the distance, and they were able to fire a flare to draw attention to their location. Astonishingly, a passing fishing trawler saw the flare and came to their rescue. Although all attempts to move my father from the dinghy to the trawler caused him the most excruciating pain, the fishermen, with no other option, picked him up and flung him onto the deck, like a 'stranded fish'—to use his own words.

Although the Spaniards did not speak English, they did manage some form of communication. Algiers was the nearest port, but its approach had been mined; and so after twelve hours, they arrived at Melilla in Spanish Morocco, where my father was hospitalised for five months.

His body bore those scars for the rest of his life—a deformed lower left leg which caused him to walk with a pronounced limp and a 'hole' in his back where the impact of the flight levers had stripped the flesh from his ribcage. My mother told me that early in their courting days, he had insisted on showing her these scars so that she knew what she would have to accept, if she chose to marry him.

The fifteenth of September became an important date in our family—not only was it the day he 'fell out of the sky,' but it was also the date he proposed to my mother fourteen years later. He wanted the date of his survival to be commemorated by this second, more positive life-changing event. Their courtship and engagement were only eight months—my gestation was longer than their entire pre-marriage relationship. I have often wondered whether they'd taken enough time to get to know one another.

When I was growing up, none of my friends had fathers who had been in the war—they were all too young. It made mine an oddity in that regard—he was in his late thirties when I was born, and the combination of his age and his injuries meant that he found it difficult to play the kind of games that younger fathers play with their children. He displayed a frailty, a delicateness that belied his military past. His blond hair and soft blue eyes were more reminiscent of a young Roger Moore than the wartime movie heroes, James Stewart or Clark Gable. Compared to my friends' fathers, he seemed so much older, different and flawed.

∽

I knocked on Bill's door, which was slightly ajar, and poked my head around the corner.

'You wanted to see me?'

Bill and Tub were sitting at the desk. 'Come in, Louise. Take a seat. We need to have a chat.' This sounded ominous. I had been at the helicopter flying school on the Sunshine Coast for five months and at forty-eight, was older than all of the other students. In fact, I was older than some of their mothers.

I had passed all seven of my ground theory subjects and was now undertaking the flying phase accompanied by either Bill, the Chief Pilot or Tub, the Senior Instructor. Between them, these men had over seventy years of flying experience. Obviously, my status as matriarch of the group had warranted the most learned of teachers.

I was there to secure my commercial pilot's licence. It was an adventure which had grown from an idea that came to me while working on a luxury island in the Seychelles only eight months earlier. Guests travelling from Mahe to Tortoise Island could choose to take a three-hour boat ride or a fifteen-minute chopper flight. Most folks would opt to fly, even though it cost a lot more. If the pilot had no guests to take back to the capital, the chopper was available for staff—it was known as the empty leg. I could easily find a genuine, or even manufactured, reason to leave the island and so I was a regular traveller.

My interest in these flying machines was not new. It had begun twenty-five years earlier when I was an Army Reservist. Our annual camp was supported by the Air Force, and we were given the opportunity to fly in Iroquois or Chinook helicopters. I was in awe of the pilots who were in control of these flights of freedom—to be able to escape the earth's bonds and take charge of their own destinies.

And as we flew over the Indian Ocean on these short excursions, I had wondered if it was a skill I could master. I had defined myself by my career in human resources (HR) for twenty-five years, but in recent times, it no longer held the same appeal. I had given my life to helping people with their problems. I was tired and drained—I had no more to give. I certainly had nothing left for myself. I wanted a new career—and I chose one that was as far removed from HR as I could imagine.

Now I had been summoned.

'Louise.' Bill paused for what seemed longer than necessary. 'We have loved having you here at Chopperline. You have been a breath of fresh air. We don't get many women here, and certainly not a woman of your age. You have worked hard, and you have fitted in well with the other students and staff.'

I had the sense that there was about to be a significant *but* heading in my direction. It turned out to be a *however*.

'However, you might have noticed that you have not yet flown solo. By this stage in your flying hours, you should have achieved this status.'

I was well aware that I was the last person in my course to take off without an instructor. Others had flown solo after only ten hours of accompanied flight—my logbook showed that I had over forty hours. I was about to become the record holder of the least wanted record at the school—the highest number of flying hours before going solo. I was embarrassed and frustrated by my failure to grasp the basics of flying. Teenagers were so far ahead of me—flying a helicopter was like manipulating the controls on an Xbox game, and they were all adept at that. I had quickly learned that being older and having more life experience did not necessarily determine one's ability to fly.

I had also taken longer than any other student to master the art of hovering. For me, the interplay between the three mechanisms required to achieve this feat was elusory. Finally, on a calm sunny day, I had managed to travel to the far side of the airfield, point the nose of the helicopter at the designated tree and remain on the spot, some twenty feet off the ground. Tub had been ecstatic.

'Oh my god. She's been kissed on the head by the hover fairy.'

I had been hailed as a conquering hero when I returned to the flight line that day.

'I know, I know. I am aware that it seems to be taking me a lot longer than others.'

'Well,' said Tub, who had spent the most time in the chopper with me, 'your problem is,' he paused, 'you do not have a single natural flying bone in your body.'

As I looked over at my sleeping father, I wondered whether I had inherited my lack of flying bones from him. Here was a man who had read, and re-read, the complete works of Shakespeare, had a passion for theatre and jazz, played chess, and in his eighties, had taught himself to speak Spanish. I wondered whether he too had been far out of his comfort zone for the entire time that he flew during the war. What had driven him to take this extraordinary decision? Was it his sense of duty that allowed him to conquer his fears?

And what was my driving force? Why had I embarked on this enterprise—so out of character and away from all that was familiar?

Back in Caloundra, the heat had risen in my cheeks, and I'd wriggled in my seat like a child in the principal's office.

'Must be something about operating machinery. My mother tells me it took three attempts for me to get my driver's licence.'

'Of course, we are very happy to keep working with you and to keep taking your money.' Bill laughed nervously at his own joke. 'It is just that we will be doing that for a really long time. We felt it was only fair to let you know so that we could discuss your options.'

'So you're telling me that I am not likely to be James Packer's next personal helicopter pilot?'

They both laughed.

'Right. So where to from here?'

'It is up to you to tell us what you want.'

'Okay. This was on my bucket list of "things to do before I die." I reckon that for me to be able to give it a tick, I need to get to solo.'

'Well, if you are up for it, so are we. We will make that the focus for the rest of your time with us.'

As I'd left Bill's office, I realised I had been squarely put in my place. I had just been told that I was failing as a student, that I was not up to the standard required and that much younger students were proving to be far more capable. As a high achiever, I ought to have been extremely disappointed. But I was not upset. In fact, I was relieved. Thank God. I had a legitimate reason to give up on this flying dream—my instructors had told me that it was the best course of action. Now I did not have to admit to anyone that I was actually terrified of flying.

Each time the earth had fallen away below my chopper, there had been no light and delicate butterflies in my stomach—more like gigantic moths pounding their furry wings against the very fabric of my inner self. It was no wonder I had not been able to master the art of flying—I'd been too busy remembering how to breathe.

As I'd wandered back to the flight line, it dawned on me that for several months, I had put myself in a situation where I was not in control. More than that—in a state of constant fear.

How on earth had I allowed that to happen—again?

MEDICAL MATTERS

There was a knock on the door. A woman entered the room pushing a trolley.

'Sorry to interrupt but it's teatime. Does your dad want a cuppa?'

His eyes opened and he tilted his head towards her. He nodded and she placed a plastic mug of a jelly-like substance on his bedside table. There was a spoon standing upright in it.

She saw my quizzical look. 'It is actually black tea, thickened to make it easier for him to swallow and digest. Would you like me to feed it to him?'

'No, that's fine. I will be able to do that.' I was surprised at my willingness to take on this role.

She left, and we were alone again.

Moving my chair closer, I picked up the tea. I took a spoonful and instinctively blew on it, ensuring that it was not too hot for his lips and his narrowed throat. He opened his mouth and swallowed, staring into my eyes.

'I can't believe you're here. I really can't believe that you're here.' It was obvious he was having difficulty accepting that after so many years, I'd come to visit him.

'Well, I am, Dad. I am really here. Now have some more tea.'

I fed him, spoonful after spoonful, until he had taken half of the contents of the cup.

'That's enough. I don't want any more.'

I wiped away traces of tea that were caught in the corner of his mouth. He smiled, a lop-sided grin, and we continued to stare at each other.

There was so much to say, but neither of us spoke. Here we were, just the two of us. Me and dad, dad and me.

I held his hand, and within a few moments, he was asleep. His breathing was so shallow that I watched him intently to ensure he was still alive. I found the state of his shrivelled and frail body to be confronting, shocking. It was as though he was shrinking into the earth, one kilogram and one centimetre at a time.

I looked over to the bookshelf and noticed another item in the bottom left-hand corner.

A stethoscope. Coiled on the shelf like a sleeping rattlesnake. This international and eternal icon of the medical profession. Worn around the necks of both genuine and celluloid medicos. A symbol of care, compassion and healing as well as knowledge, authority and power.

Following his terrible accident and the miraculous story of his survival, my father had decided he wanted to repay society, to give to others the gift he had received in Morocco. And so, from the age of thirty, he had trained for many years to become a doctor.

Like flying, I wondered how difficult this must have been for him—having to understand the sciences required to pass the necessary subjects. Anatomy, physiology, biology—all were new to him, and he'd found their concepts difficult to grasp. But eventually, he qualified in 1957 and became a general practitioner in the north of England.

We were always conscious of our role as the children of a doctor which came with a great sense of duty and responsibility. In those days, patients would ring the doctors' home numbers to make appointments or request an out-of-hours visit. The phone needed to be monitored at all times and answered with the precision of a medical centre receptionist, even if you were only seven years old.

However, England's national health system—characterised by long hours and an impossible daily patient workload—was taking its toll on an older physician, his wife and young family. As I leafed through the papers on his shelf, I saw a copy of the typed letter my father sent to the Clerk of the Executive Council for Sheffield tendering his resignation and his reasons for leaving the UK. It was dated September 1966.

It is now quite clear that the medical profession can no longer hope for either understanding or constructive co-operation from a Minister of Health who deals with a worsening situation by verbal attacks on a section of the profession....

My decision will involve my wife and I in severance from our native country, relatives and friends, with a multitude of inconveniences associated with so major a removal. I am forty-six years old and have four young children. Anyone, the Minister included, who thinks such a move to be a light-hearted spree is totally devoid of imagination…

In 1967, when I was eight, we emigrated to Australia as Ten Pound Poms on a programme implemented by the Australian and New Zealand governments after World War II. The scheme provided assisted passage to nearly one million suitably qualified migrants from the British Isles and selected European countries. The name was derived from the fact that each migrating adult had to pay only ten pounds for the trip to their new country. We were required to remain in Australia for a minimum of two years, bonded to our sponsoring employer. If we left before that time, we would have to repay the full cost of the travel, an amount of two hundred and forty pounds, the equivalent of a year's wages for my father.

Once all the research had been done, there was never any question we would leave England. The more relaxed lifestyle, constant blue skies and warm weather, the fact dad would be working as a geriatrician in a country Victorian hospital, rather than in general practice, all contributed to the 'rightness' of my parents' decision.

When my father ceased being a general practitioner and moved into a hospital environment, he was required to be less hands-on with patients. I thought this was a very good idea. Just before we left the UK, I had experienced my father's skills with 'needle and thread.' There was a building site next door to our house and as I climbed over the jagged concrete pieces, I managed to inflict a deep cut to my right calf. I ran home with blood pouring down my leg, and my mother rushed me to dad's surgery.

He injected anaesthetic around the wound—with far too many needle jabs as far as I was concerned—and proceeded to sew up my almond-shaped gash. Fifty years later, the scar remains almond-shaped. The sides of the wound had not been brought together, which would have been the correct procedure for this type of laceration. Many years later, he admitted that it was 'not his finest piece of handiwork.' I look at my scar, and it reminds me of the man who was once again out of his comfort zone.

Now here I was with him, my father, the medical practitioner who in different circumstances would have wanted to know if I was 'enjoying good health.' He would have been interested personally and professionally. But neither of us initiated this topic of conversation. We had each received treatment for our similar but different medical conditions, but it was life-threatening only to him.

I did not want to raise my medical history with him. For some reason, I did not want to worry him. Why did that still matter so much? For so many years throughout my childhood and young adult life, I had seen it as my responsibility to ensure that no-one had any reason to be worried about anything.

While we were growing up, we seemed a set of flawless kinfolk to clueless, admiring onlookers. My siblings and I did well at school, played in the right sporting teams and took part in all the proper extracurricular activities. The father was a doctor, and the wife was a stay-at-home mum. We were people who minded their own business and caused no ripples in society. Just like those robotic wives, we were the perfect Stepford family.

Fluorescent light entered the crevices of my eyelids, forcing them into a blinking reality. Blurred images appeared, taking shape as though being focussed through binoculars.

Sensation returned and I felt a tingling in my fingers and toes. Nausea travelled the full length of my body, into my throat and exploded through my mouth as convulsing spasms lifted my body off the bed.

How had it come to this? I was thousands of miles from home, in the first month of a year-long holiday to the UK, as part of a twenty-first birthday present to myself.

'Did you get your period, darling? I know you said it was late this month?'

'Yes, Mum, all good. Nothing to worry about.' A fortnight before I left Australia, that lie had struggled to leave my tongue, like an insect trying to escape from a Venus flytrap. I was about to head off on my first solo adventure to the far side of the world, and I was going to have to deal with the consequences of a missed period—alone.

Three weeks earlier, I had arrived in London and was staying with family friends in Golders Green—

Peter Shire had been my parents' best man and he had offered to provide a base for me until I was able to move to the south side of the city to live with my great-aunt Gwen.

In order to achieve my current subterfuge, I had managed to convince the Shires I was visiting Gwen and had told Gwen that I was staying at the Shires, and as they did not know one another, I was able to spend the night in this unlikely location, with my secret intact.

Too late, a nurse appeared with a kidney dish. She took a towel and wiped my face, then mopped the bed clothes. Seeing my embarrassment, she said, 'Don't worry—that's quite normal. It's just a reaction to the anaesthetic. You'll feel better soon.'

I stared at the ceiling, gradually sensing the presence of others. Like pupae in their chrysalises, young women lay swaddled in crisp white sheets with woollen army blankets pulled tight across the single metal-framed beds, which stretched from one end of the ward to the other. We looked like casualties in a scene from a World War II movie. Like me, they too were prone, staring above, not daring to glance sideways, in case we caught one another's gaze. This was a place of anonymity, no eye contact, no conversations. We came and went—we were never here.

I touched the exterior of my body; I visited the interior. I was feeling—what? I expected to feel sadness, shame at my decision, regretful, appalled—surely that was how I was meant to be feeling. But I was none of those things. I was relieved and felt lighter, in spite of the heavy padding between my legs. The anxiety, guilt and confusion I had borne since discovering the consequence of that weekend of unbridled, unsafe sex, with a man I barely knew, had passed.

I was convinced of the rightness of my choice. I was convinced then. I remain convinced still.

Over the years, I've pondered the enormity of my choice. I wonder if that tiny soul lives on in another, because that was its destiny.

ACTING THE PART

'I might break wind from time to time.'

Stirring from his slumber, and with his eyes still closed, I wondered if I had heard him correctly.

'What was that, Dad?'

'I might break wind from time to time. I do apologise in advance for that.'

'Well, um, that's fine, Dad. Remember what your mother always used to say? That epitaph from an old headstone? "Where e'er you be, let your wind blow free, for 'twas the wind that killeth me."' As soon as I said it, I realised that a conversation about bottled-up flatulence leading to one's untimely demise was probably not the best conversation to have with an aging father in the final stages of his life.

'I am so sorry that I keep dropping off to sleep. I am not very good company.'

He seemed disappointed in himself.

'That's fine, Dad. I have all afternoon to be with you. I have nowhere else to be.' That was true. This was the only place I wanted to be. 'We can talk about everything … or nothing … whatever we want.'

His eyes watered, and he smiled. 'You are a good scout.'

'A good scout, eh? Well, I suppose I am. Never thought of myself as a good scout.' I was conscious that I was overemphasizing my words and that they sounded patronizing, as though speaking to a child or to a person whose first language was not English. I was nervous and I was over-compensating.

I resorted to activity. 'Do you want me to wipe your eyes for you?'

'Yes, please. That would be good.'

I took another tissue, dabbed the corners of his eyes and then, very gently, wiped it across both eyelids. The paper-thin skin would not have survived a more enthusiastic approach.

'I am so sorry that I wasn't prepared to … to greet you.'

'That's okay, Dad. I think it was always going to be a bit of a surprise … this meeting. I don't think either of us could have ever been really prepared.'

We were silent, once again feeling the space, the lost years between us.

While he dozed off again, I glanced over to the bookshelf. There were four photographs on display—one I had never seen before of my father and his two older brothers. He was sitting on a stool as they stood on either side—he wore a dress and seemed to be six months old. That would have been 1920. There was another of the three brothers, taken about sixty years later in country Victoria. It must have been a significant occasion—the middle brother lived in New Zealand

and rarely visited. Another photo was of my parents on their wedding day. My mother so beautiful, with her eighteen-inch waist, and my father, so handsome.

There was only one photo that included any of his four children—one of him and my youngest brother, Mark, taken on Mark's wedding day. We had come together as a family for this fourth and final family wedding. The speeches had been made; the photos had been taken. All the prerequisites of a happy family gathering completed.

But I wondered if it was actually the following day that stood out for him—that signified the divide between *before* and *after*. I had come to the celebration with a clear purpose in mind—I knew that I would tell my father what had been building up for years. As my family celebrated in the courtyard of a Brisbane pub, I told him the words that I needed him to hear.

Seeing this photo, I needed to regroup—the floods of tears unsettled me. I had felt courageous and strong in making this visit, and crying made me feel the opposite. I had been stoic all these years and had worn that stoicism as a mark of pride. I couldn't bear the thought of losing it now.

I wandered into his bathroom and splashed water on my face. *Get a grip*, I berated myself. *For God's sake, the visit has only just begun.*

I need not have worried. When I returned, his eyes were still closed.

I noticed a red manila folder on his bookshelf, full of papers. I picked it up and flicked through them. There were all kinds of historical family materials and pages of handwritten notes.

ACT 1 — ACTING THE PART

I came across a program from a play, *The Cave Dwellers*, performed by the Gosford Players in 1971. Its lettering and crude images pointed to a time well before computers and laser printers, when amateur dramatic societies produced their programs on typewriters and copied them on Gestetner machines.

And suddenly, I was transported back in time.

From early childhood, I shared my father's passion for the theatre. We both kept programs from theatrical and musical performances. As I sat with this programme in my hands, I wondered why he had kept this particular piece of memorabilia, especially as we had both performed in so many plays and musicals over the years. It had travelled with him from Terrigal to Bendigo in the 1970s, to Echuca in the 1980s and finally, to Geelong where we were now.

Then I noticed that both my father's and my name appeared in the cast list. Perhaps he had kept this program because it was the first time we had appeared on stage together. I was twelve and had played two roles—the 'Young Queen' and 'Woman with Dog.' Taking role-playing to the extreme, my father had played the role of 'The Father.'

It was in Gosford that I had seen my first live musical—a production of *Rose Marie* by the local theatrical society in 1970. It is an operetta, written in the 1920s, with themes of murder and forbidden love. To an outsider, it might have seemed an odd choice for a twelve-year-old's birthday outing.

But by then, my childhood had been anything but typical.

Between 1970 and 1972, from the ages of twelve to fourteen, I became a human teabag, steeped in the world of plays and musical theatre. While young Jewish girls of the same age were preparing for their batmitzvah and learning the scriptures, I was memorizing scripts. The theatre became my temple.

I would hang around the stage door after a performance, an adoring sycophant, hoping to catch a glimpse, a signature, from my new-found heroes. One of my most vivid captures was after I saw that ground-breaking, life-changing production—*Jesus Christ Superstar*.

As I sat in the theatre and watched this spectacular, I knew that musical theatre would never be the same again. Lloyd Webber and Rice were the new Rodgers and Hammerstein. This modern pair of musical creators heralded a brave new world. Instead of 'clambakes' and 'enchanted evenings,' we were hearing those irreverent words, '*Hey, Jesus, prove to me that you're divine. Change my water into wine.*' For someone who had been an avid attendee of Sunday school for many years, this felt blasphemous and wicked.

In a move that would be impossible these days, I went backstage to secure Jon English's autograph— the most extraordinary Judas, so tall and with those dark, deep-set eyes; a human praying mantis, who certainly gave the impression that he decided whether or not you got to keep your head. That was an awe-filled moment infused with the smell of sweat, both his and mine.

Holding this program in my hands in my father's small room, I realised that all these roles were about identity and finding your true self. Looking back, the irony seemed so evident.

When I was in my final year of school in Bendigo, I performed the climactic final scene of *Roots*—a play by Arnold Wesker. It was an eight-hundred-word monologue by Beatie, a young woman learning who she is and what she believes, as she moves away from her traditional rural origins. I was about to leave country Victoria for university in Melbourne.

Beatie was standing in her own truth—and finally, at the age of eighteen, so was I.

The most memorable play of all was *Pygmalion*, which I'd performed in when I was almost sixteen.

The curtain had opened with a flourish, and we had stood, hand in hand, tall and proud. Henry Higgins to my left, Colonel Pickering to my right. We raised our clasped hands high in the air and dramatically folded at the waist. The school-hall audience clapped and cheered, wolf-whistled, rose to their feet for a standing ovation. With all this adulation, we turned and smiled at one another, exhausted but thrilled at this reception, this ultimate acknowledgement of our efforts. We bowed again.

My eyes had scanned the crowd. I wondered if he had come tonight—it was our last performance after all.

And suddenly, there he was. The milling crowd parted as he had moved towards me. This moment would be awkward, formal. His public persona was not one that exuded an easy warmth.

I had held my breath. The last few months flashed by in a moment—the hours of rehearsal after a long day at school, practicing and perfecting that cockney accent, so vital to the role. The transition—'in Hertford, Hereford and Hampshire, hurricanes hardly ever happen'—over and over, to convince the audience and myself of the transformation Eliza had made.

He'd stood in front of me. 'You were bloody marvellous.'

He never swore.

I'd exhaled. That had been all I needed—I'd met his standard. Once again, I had secured his approval.

Our blue eyes had met.

'Thanks,' I'd said quietly. 'Thanks, Dad.'

~

I became aware of music coming from somewhere in his room. A CD player was sitting on the bookshelf, and I realised it must have been playing quietly since before I arrived. As I focused on the melody, suddenly, I began to laugh out of sheer incredulity and the release of huge tension. Of all the songs in the world, this had to be playing on this day, in this place?

'Dad, can you hear the song that's playing? Did you choose it? I cannot believe what I am hearing.' He was awake and straining to hear the tune.

'What is it? I can't make it out.'

I wondered if the nurses chose this particular CD, knowing of my visit. *That was most unlikely*, I told myself. It was just random, the kind of thing that happens because the universe likes to mess with our heads.

I got up to look at the CD cover. It was a compilation of songs by Cole Porter, a favourite of my father's. The singer was Mary Martin, who I had heard many times during my youth in early recordings of shows such as *Oklahoma* and *The Sound of Music*. She was catapulted to fame in the late 1930s because of this very song.

Now here she was, in my father's retirement home, singing, 'My Heart Belongs to Daddy.'

MUSICAL INTERLUDES

The words of the song played in my ears. She was telling her man that even though he might be 'swell,' her heart belonged to 'daddy,' because he treated her 'so well.'

Music had been important to my father. He was not a musician, although he tinkled the ivories in an ad-hoc fashion. His musical passions were varied but consistently conservative. He loved classical composers such as Beethoven (his favourite), Mozart, Tchaikovsky, Bach, Brahms and Chopin. Jazz made a regular appearance in the form of Benny Goodman and Fats Waller. There was Cole Porter and the Gershwin brothers, as well as Gilbert and Sullivan, and Rogers and Hammerstein. At times, this musical diet was so constant, we children felt like force-fed geese expected to consume as much as possible in order to create the most perfect *foie gras* of appreciation.

So I had learned to play the piano. My parents regarded that instrument as good musical grounding. Over the years, I worked my way through a number of practical and theory exams. Although I was not a gifted player, I achieved a standard acceptable to me—and them. Later, I wondered if the discipline required to learn scales, for example, was a metaphor for life—sometimes you climb and climb, only to fall back down and have to start all over again.

Others in the family were more talented on that instrument, so I decided I would learn the classical guitar. I enjoyed this new challenge, and with no other guitar players in the family, there were no comparisons to be made. I had lessons from the age of twelve and was able to give the impression that I could play more proficiently than was in fact the case. This became evident when we moved to another state, and I went to audition with a new teacher. I played my most complicated, most rehearsed piece for him, and he was delighted to take me as a student. However, during my first lesson, as we worked through my repertoire, he had a puzzled look on his face.

'Oh. Hmmm. Well, this is disappointing. When you played the Albinez piece for me, I thought you were at a much higher standard. Now I see that you simply rote learnt it, and your skills are not nearly as advanced as I thought. We have a lot of work to do.'

It appeared I had become adept at faking it 'til I made it. I had been instructed in the art of deception from such an early age that it now permeated my life. I thought that as long as no-one was getting hurt, it really didn't matter.

I had yet to learn how it might be hurting me.

At the age of fourteen, I entered a classical instrument solo competition at the Bendigo Festival in the City Hall. There were only six of us in the category with a first prize of $6 and a second prize of $2. I won neither.

My interest in classical guitar began to wane, and I decided to move on to a new hobby. I sold my beautiful instrument, trading it in for an electric guitar, complete with a small amplifier. I joined an all-girl group with a few like-minded teenagers. We met on the weekends and played a range of songs that included the entire Joan Baez songbook, the Seekers and such classics as 'Burning Bridges' from the movie *Kelly's Heroes* and 'House of the Rising Sun' by The Animals. It didn't matter that these were men's songs. We just liked the tunes and thought we were so cool, with our two guitarists and a drummer.

I also sang. I was an average soprano and always sounded much better accompanied by a choir, than as a soloist. The school madrigal group was well regarded, and we travelled around Victoria singing at events and festivals.

On one occasion, I was required to sing a duet with a far more talented soprano. Her voice was so true and pure, and I worried that my average performance would detract from her flawless one. I decided that I would just make sure that I stood as near to her as possible. Our bodies were so close that people would have thought we were preparing for a three-legged race.

'Turn that cacophony down! Is that what is passing for music these days? Beethoven would be rolling over in his grave. His Symphony Number 5 had that four-note combination hundreds of years before these long-haired gits. I never thought that I would be hearing that type of music in this house.'

His voice trailed off as he wandered back along the corridor of our home.

I lay on my bed and listened to his disappearing, disappointed footsteps. I didn't have the nerve to remind him that 'Roll Over Beethoven' was a popular song already recorded by Chuck Berry, the Beatles and the Electric Light Orchestra. I didn't care what he thought. I was tired of being so far behind the times. My upbringing had seemed so narrow, influenced by my conservative parents. I had been fed on a lifelong diet of the classics as well as jazz, musicals and light opera (that annoying 'modern Major General'). At the age of fourteen, I decided I needed to take a stand, to assert my right to listen to the music of my generation.

So I finally bought myself an album the in-crowd at school had been talking about. And I was playing it at full volume in the privacy of my own room.

It was 1973, the band was Deep Purple, and the song was 'Smoke on the Water.' That twelve-beat guitar riff was so powerful—'bam, bam, bam, ba, ba, ba bam, bam bam bam, ba bam.' I banged my head like a demented rock star. My choice of music was the closest I ever felt to being rebellious as a child and young adult.

I had never spoken back to my parents. I never broke whatever curfew they set. In all activities, I was determined to set a good example as the eldest of all my siblings.

I always took the responsibility of being the eldest seriously.

For me, this quirk of the birth order was ordained by a power greater than ourselves and was therefore sacrosanct.

As Princess Elizabeth said in 1947, 'I declare before you all that my whole life, whether it be long or short, shall be devoted to your service.' Like the queen in waiting, I had been given a lifelong job, and I never once shirked the responsibility I had to protect my younger siblings. Even at my own expense.

KISS ME GOODNIGHT, SERGEANT MAJOR

There was a knock on the door. A young man leaned into the room. He gestured towards dad.

'It's lunchtime. Would you like me to take your father down to the dining room?'

Already? Time was passing more quickly than I expected.

'Is it okay if I sit with him while he has his lunch?'

'Sure. He can feed himself, but sometimes he prefers us to do that. Perhaps he'd like you to feed him today.'

He unlocked the brakes on the reclining chair. 'Ready for some lunch…?' The young man used my father's name.

My father nodded, and the young carer gently steered him out of the room.

I had always been self-conscious about my father's name. It was odd and old-fashioned, and when I was growing up, nobody else had a father with the same name. If I had known then that its origin was Greek and meant royal or kingly, I might have been more generous in my thinking. But to me, it was the name of a children's hand puppet and a ridiculous hotel manager created by John Cleese, who thrashed cars and insulted the entire German nation. It has always remained an oddity to me.

We headed down the corridor, through the lounge and arrived at the communal dining room. As we approached my father's table, members of staff spoke in hushed tones and nodded in our direction. It seemed my appearance was a talking point, perhaps because this was the first time my father had received a female visitor.

I moved to where dad had been wheeled beside the table and pulled up a chair.

Without knowing exactly what I would encounter on this extraordinary day, I had anticipated that we might be in this very situation—lunchtime in the retirement home. Again, I had rehearsed this scenario in my mind. My early theatrical training had taught me that a rehearsal is never wasted.

'Would you like me to feed you, Dad?' I slipped into the role of dutiful, caring daughter. It was a character I had played for many years, and in spite of everything, I found myself reconciled to the stereotype.

He nodded but seemed agitated by something he saw on the table in front of him. He lifted his hand out from under the blanket and pointed at the place mat.

'What do you need, Dad?'

With extreme effort, he managed, 'Put the fork on the left and the spoon on the right.'

They were sitting together on the right-hand side of the mat. I placed them as he requested, even though he would not be using these implements.

In that moment, I was transported back to the dinner table of my childhood. My siblings and I took turns to set the table, and that setting always had to be the same—the fork to the left, the knife to the right, with the soup spoon to the right of that and the dessert spoon across the top. The cutlery needed to be neat and straight. We would not have dared do otherwise.

To this day, I place the stamp on an envelope in precisely the top right-hand corner, perfectly aligned to the edges, just as he always did. These habits were such a metaphor of our perfect, regimented lives in which we would not dream of stepping outside the lines—we never did place the stamp askew. Not then and not now.

'Would you like me to feed you, Dad?'

He smiled and nodded.

I began to offer him small spoonfuls of his lunch—mushy peas, sieved carrots, mashed potatoes and pulverized meatloaf. A great deal of care had been taken by the home to ensure that the food was prepared so he could easily eat it.

Feeding dad was a bizarre, unique experience. I felt superior. Even a bit smug. For the first time in my life, in my father's presence, I was completely in control. I determined the size of the spoonful, the combination of foods, the frequency with which I offered the spoon to his mouth. Responsible for his nourishment, feeling his dependence on me, even for a few minutes, I felt a reversal. In that moment, I cared only for his welfare, conscious of his fragile state (although the thought of proffering an empty spoon did fleetingly cross my mind).

After lunch, I took charge of the wheeled chair and we headed back to his room. Other residents and staff waved or said hello as he passed. He might have been one of the more recent inhabitants of the home, but he was also one of the oldest. It was obvious he was held in high regard, respected as an elder of their tribe.

I carefully positioned him beside the bed and realised that during the short journey from the dining room, he had again drifted off to sleep.

My gaze returned to the bookshelf, and I noticed that his World War II medals were sitting beside his flight logbook, and the yearbook from his time spent learning to fly in Alabama seventy-five years earlier.

I too had served in the armed forces and received the Australian Defence Medal which I wear with great pride on Anzac Day, a reminder of my time in the Army Reserve.

When I was nineteen, in 1978, I was at university in Melbourne living at Queen's College when one of the other residents, Thomas, had said, 'You should come and join the Army Reserve. It is great fun, and we parade on a Wednesday night from 7pm to 10pm.'

Marching up and down a parade ground for three hours, at night, in the middle of the week, did not sound like my kind of fun.

However, I was curious, and the following Wednesday evening, I accompanied him to the Melbourne University Regiment in Carlton. I soon learned that the term *parade* referred to the weekly time during which all manner of military skills could be acquired, from weaponry to drill, radio communications to driving trucks. I was hooked from that very moment and joined on the spot. It felt so right—an homage to my maternal grandfather, who served as a senior officer in World War II at the age of thirty-two and was among the three-hundred thousand evacuated from Dunkirk. And of course, to my father, the pilot.

At the time, I did not think it odd that as a woman, I was following in these masculine footsteps. I was in my second year at university and had arranged my timetable so that my first lecture of the day was at 2pm which enabled late nights, drinking port and eating Tim Tams. I imagined that this newly instilled military life would add the discipline I lacked.

Over the next nine years, it became a regular commitment of one night a week, one weekend a month, and fortnight training camps at least twice a year. I progressed from private to corporal, and then undertook officer training, a process which took twelve months. Many of my family members, including my father, attended my graduation parade. Once again, he and I were on common ground. As I stood to attention with my fellow recipients and received my commission from the reviewing officer, I saw him also standing, his arms smartly by his side, as he would have done on parade forty years earlier.

Another achievement, another opportunity to make him proud.

Was there no end to this game of charades?

~

'You have the most amazing blue eyes,' she said as she moved from her side of the desk and perched herself on its corner, peering into my face. I sat back in my seat. This did not fit with the conversation we had been having. She was my platoon commander, and I was one of her thirty-five female recruits; and we had, until that point, been talking about my military career ambitions.

'Ma'am' had been late arriving at the camp. She had waited to receive her commission as a lieutenant before she could take up the role as our leader. She was only a couple of years older than me, and her shiny new 'pips' stood out on her shiny new, custom-made uniform. She was a round person—round head, round face and a significantly round body. In army fatigues, she looked like a green version of the Stay Puft Marshallow Man from the *Ghostbusters* movie.

Suddenly, she launched herself towards me and pressed her lips onto mine, hard. I did not move, could not move. She was Jabba the Hutt; I was Princess Leia, her captive. She pulled away and said, 'So what did you think of that?'

'Um,' I fumbled, 'I like boys, actually.'

'Well, if you ever change your mind...' she said as she returned to her side of the desk and sat down.

Her words followed me like a vapour trail as I stumbled out of the room, heading for my hut. Ashamed, confused, angry—but silent.

What was wrong with me? Why had I not spoken out, slapped her, stormed out of her office? For God's sake, she was my commanding officer. Why was I not reporting her to the authorities?

As I sat on my bed, with its perfect hospital corners and the stripes of the blanket in complete alignment, I had a dawning realisation. Clearly, I was branded. I had a subcutaneous tattoo on my forehead that could be detected by those who were looking, like a flashing neon sign.

'Secret-Keeper.'

GOING TO THE MOVIES

The retirement home was quiet after the lunch service, and all the residents had been returned to their rooms. It was time for their afternoon naps, just as toddlers and preschoolers are required to take their blankie and find a spot on the floor to lay their head and hopefully go to sleep.

I looked at my father's sleeping face and once again, checked his imperceptible breaths. So dependent on others, so childlike, such innocence—did we truly come full circle?

How was I feeling about this visit? He knew I was there, but his capacity for conversation was almost gone. What did I think we would talk about? Did I really want to raise issues from the past, the reason for our estrangement? And given the purpose of my visit, what would that achieve?

Whatever the limitations, I was pleased I was there. He knew I had come after all these years. He seemed to grasp its significance, and the rest would take care of itself. I put my questioning on hold, resting it on the bookshelf with the other memories.

The array of books was not extensive, especially for a man who had been an avid reader all his life. The poems of TS Eliot, Bill Bryson's *A Short History of Nearly Everything,* Alain de Botton's *Religion for Atheists,* and of course, Shakespeare—so many of his plays (I counted sixteen) and even different editions of the same play.

As a child, I was aware of his passion for the bard. In fact, a diary note from my 1972 journal had the line, 'Dad read Shakespeare.'

He loved to read aloud favourite phrases or entire scenes. I would be required to sit quietly and listen appreciatively. Of course, I had no idea what any of it meant, but I did like the poetic and musical qualities of the words. Dad would finish his oration, expecting me to have grasped the magnificence and talent of the playwright. I found it best to just nod and smile.

It was also important to him that I understood the nuances of the writing and the fact that words from the seventeenth century were used in a different context from those of today. So Juliet's, 'Wherefore art thou, Romeo?' was not a question concerning his whereabouts, but why his name was Romeo, a Montague, and therefore forbidden to Juliet, a Capulet. He would be furious in performances of the play where an actor clearly did not understand the true meaning of the question.

'The emphasis should be on the word *Romeo* and not on the word *wherefore.* Why do these people keep getting that wrong?'

This very specific criticism summed up his pedantic nature.

Whilst the Shakespearean plays on his bookshelf were no surprise, I found the mix of other novels to be so varied that I wondered whether the man I thought I knew had somehow changed in the years we had not seen one another.

Once more, the bookshelf provoked recollections of childhood events and times we had spent together. *1001 Movies You Must See Before You Die* stood out in large gold letters. How long had he owned this book and had he been making an effort to do as the cover suggested? Now that he was in the final stages of his life, this title seemed to be urging him to an impossible challenge.

Movies had been another of our common interests. A copy of Leonard Maltin's *Movie Guide* has never been far from my fingertips. It was published every two years when I was a teenager, and I would get the updated version either for my birthday or Christmas.

In fact, my parents went to the movies on their wedding night. They saw the musical *Seven Brides for Seven Brothers*. Well, I suppose it did have a wedding theme.

The first movie I ever saw was *Mary Poppins* when I was seven. I was convinced I was Jane Banks and that I should be the one floating around the ceiling with Mary. I disappeared into the celluloid for every glorious minute of that adventure.

And there were so many songs. I loved the music and dancing even though Bert was portrayed by Dick van Dyke with a very poor cockney accent.

ACT 1 — GOING TO THE MOVIES

Since that first musical movie, I had an uncanny knack for learning songs as a child and to this day, am word perfect in all the songs from all the musicals I ever saw while growing up yet have no conscious memory of trying to learn them. I must have simply inhaled them.

Over the years, going to the movies became one of the things I did alone with dad. However well-intentioned his choices, they were sometimes quite inappropriate for a child.

As I was doing karate in my early teens, he decided to take me to the latest Bruce Lee movie, *Enter the Dragon*. It was 1973, and it was to be Lee's last movie. At that time, these movies were badly dubbed from Chinese to English; and like the *Samurai* television series, the movement of the mouths did not match with the spoken words.

This movie was entirely unsuitable for a fourteen-year-old. It provided examples of the most extreme forms of martial arts, with a degree of violence and body count that I had certainly never seen at that age. It bore no resemblance to my weekly karate sessions at the local church hall. Up until that point, the most painful aspect of my martial art was having to remove the many splinters which my flat feet sucked up from the ancient wooden floors.

As we flinched and winced at every horrendous fight and each bloodied antagonist that was dispatched by Lee, I wondered what he had been thinking. Clearly, he had done no research into this movie and its suitability for either of us. It was a martial arts movie, I was studying karate, so he'd assumed it would be a fit. My sleep patterns were significantly disturbed for many nights, long after the credits had rolled.

But this was his pattern. He was a man who made inappropriate choices by exposing me to aspects of the world I wasn't ready for—and never would be.

ACT 2
FLASHBACK

THE DARKNESS

'So many children are dead. It's awful. They were in their classrooms—school had just started for the day. And then they were covered by the mudslide. It is truly awful.'

My mother had tears in her eyes, and she was brushing her hands up and down her apron, as though trying to remove non-existent specks of flour. What had happened to make her so sad? Dad had just come home, and they were talking in the kitchen.

'I reckon they'll find out the mining company was to blame. All those piles of spoil sitting above the town—it was only a matter of time. And after all that rain they've been having across Wales. Terrible, just terrible.'

Wales was where we went for our summer holidays. We used to stay on a farm, on the island of Anglesey, with family friends. They had children who were similar in age to us, and because it was a working farm, we were encouraged to get involved in the daily activities, which included the milking. I found the cows incredibly intimidating (and had no desire to step in freshly created cow pats), so I preferred to climb over the hay bales in the huge barn, not far from the house. It was a great place to create cubbies and hide, well away from the farmyard chores. There was also a small shed where we would play schools. The daylight would barely find its way through the murky windows, and we would have to spend time removing last year's dust from the chairs and desks. There was a blackboard and chalk at the front, and as I was the oldest, I would take charge of the class. I loved telling the others what to do, in my best teacher's voice.

On sunny days, we would take our buckets and spades to the beach at Benllech and build sandcastles with fabulous moats. If the weather cooled, we would visit the town of Beaumaris and run around the ruins of its ancient castle.

Wales was a good place, a fun place. What was the very bad thing that had happened?

The mudslide had covered many streets and buildings in the town of Aberfan, in particular, a school at the foot of the hill. Over a hundred children and dozens of adults had been killed by this wall of mud and debris. When people spoke of this event in the following weeks and months, it was known as the *disaster*.

The town was never the same again. Years later, this dreadful event would be referred to as the mistake that cost a village its children. It had lost its innocence—and its innocents.

This loss of innocence was just like the dose of measles I had recently contracted—it was catching.

Sadly, our family was familiar with loss, and especially the loss of children.

My adopted brother Mark was welcomed as an early Christmas present in late 1962. Jeffrey and I were happy to have another sibling as my mother had lost both a baby girl, Rachel, and a baby boy, Stephen, within eighteen months of each other. Both had died on the same day they had been born.

Many years later, my mother revealed that she had taken a new drug to treat her extreme cases of morning sickness. I'm certain this new drug was thalidomide, responsible for severe birth defects in thousands of children born in the late 1950s and early 1960s. It is estimated that the total number of embryos affected by its use was as many as ten thousand, of which forty percent had died around the time of birth.

She'd also suffered at least one miscarriage in amongst these four births. Her sense of cumulative loss must have been overwhelming.

Three years later, mum fell pregnant, and thankfully, my perfectly healthy sister was born in 1966. Our family of six was complete.

My mother, the nurse married to a doctor, would have rationalised that not all pregnancies result in joy and happiness. She'd have known that the chances of my brother's and sister's survival were remote, and that their disabilities would have led to an extremely poor quality of life. Rationally, logically and medically, their passing may have been a blessing.

But as a woman and mother, she never got the support she needed for the post-traumatic stress that she must have experienced. 'Keep calm and carry on' was her mantra, just as the Ministry of Information poster had encouraged during her childhood war years.

With four children under the age of eight, she had no time to grieve for the children she had lost because she had to care for the children she had. She had undergone unimaginable heartache and must have been physically and emotionally spent.

I have often wondered if this was the 'perfect storm' of circumstances that contributed to what happened next.

I clambered up the stairs to my bedroom at the very top of the house. I had cleaned my teeth and now it was time to say my prayers. I knelt beside the bed and placed my hands together in front of my chest. I was going to a Catholic school, and they were quite insistent about bedtime prayers. And besides, my favourite Winnie the Pooh books were a reminder that children should practice this nighttime ritual.

Little Boy kneels at the foot of the bed,
Droops on the little hands little gold head.
Hush! Hush! Whisper who dares!
Christopher Robin is saying his prayers.

I took a deep breath. 'God bless mummy and daddy. God bless my brothers and my new sister. God bless grandma and grandpa and the grandma who lives in New Zealand. And all my aunts and uncles and cousins.'

Then I said the Lord's Prayer, which I had recently learned by heart, and I climbed into bed. After a while, mum came up the stairs and kissed me goodnight.

'Sleep tight, darling.' She switched off the bedside lamp and left me in a sea of darkness.

I reminded my seven-year-old self that I was very brave, sleeping by myself, in the attic. It seemed to be a world away from the rest of the family, and it was very quiet.

I closed my eyes and fell asleep.

I was wakened by a sound, the creak of a floorboard on the stair. I had heard these creaks before. It was an old house, and sometimes it just made noises all by itself. I told myself that this was all part of my adventure. I had wanted to come and sleep in the attic, and I was going to have to get used to the old house making its noises.

Then I saw it. A darkness moving around the room. A shadow, whose faint outline I could see as the rising moon crossed over the garret windows. I wondered what it could be. Was it really there or was I imagining it?

The Darkness settled by the side of my bed and gently, very gently, began to turn back my bedclothes. I held my breath. Was this really happening? Was I having a nightmare? Perhaps I would wake up in a minute and The Darkness would be gone. I opened my mouth, but nothing came out—not a sound.

'Sshhh, sshhh,' said The Darkness. 'Everything is all right. We are just going to have a cuddle, but we cannot tell anyone. This will be our little secret. Secrets are fun, aren't they? And this will be just ours. Yours and mine.'

The Darkness's voice was familiar, so very familiar—but not like this, not without the lights. Not as a talking shadow.

It was now lying in the bed, pressing its shadowy self against my side. My nightie was lifted above my waist; and I felt its wispy fingers gliding over my body, touching me, stroking me. No one had ever touched me like this before. But I told myself there was no need to be scared. I knew The Darkness's voice, and it was reassuring and kind.

The Darkness breathed heavily and began shuddering beside me. Then it was silent and still.

'Remember, our special secret. You cannot tell anyone, ever.'

And then it was gone. Down the creaking staircase.

As I lay alone in my bed, I remembered the rest of Christopher Robin's song.

And what was the other I had to say?
I said 'Bless Daddy,' so what can it be?
Oh! Now I remember it. God bless Me.

MOVING TO AUSTRALIA

M-E-D (breath) I-T-E (breath) double R-A (breath) N-E-A-N.

Mediterranean—it seemed such a long, difficult word to spell when I was eight years old. The only way to manage it was to break it down into these four components.

We might have been on a five-week voyage from the UK to Australia, but our parents were determined that the basic schooling skills we had already learned would not be lost. And so, we would be given spelling tasks each day and would have to recite our times tables, all the way up to '12 times 12 is 144.'

These school-like exercises did not detract from the fact that we were on the most amazing adventure. We were leaving the UK and moving across the world. Even as an eight-year-old, I knew this was hugely significant. There were a lot of adult conversations and meetings. We had to get our photo taken as a family for the immigration documentation. As I look at that old photo, I see such excitement and anticipation on my face. Even at that age, I was up for an adventure, a change, anything out of the ordinary. Leaving my usual routine behind seemed like a very good idea. This sense of new beginnings and new hope conjured up a new world of possibilities. It was good to imagine that our old lives were being left behind in the 'old' country.

We were travelling so far. Perhaps The Darkness would not be able to find me.

In February 1967, we travelled to Southampton and boarded an Italian liner, the *Angelina Lauro*. Throngs of people climbed the steep angular gangplank that led to the arrival deck of the ship. However, our accommodation (another word we were required to spell over and over so that to this day, I take its misspelling as a personal affront) was down in the lower levels of the ship.

We had a cabin with four beds—two sets of double bunks. Originally, it had been arranged that my father was to travel in another cabin with three men—all strangers. The rest of the family were to fit into these bunk beds. However, this arrangement did not suit my parents, so dad moved back into the cabin with the rest of us. This meant that my brothers slept 'top to tail' in one bunk, and my one-year-old sister slept in a tiny cot. This was how the six of us fitted into a four-bed cabin for the five-week trip to Australia.

We left from Southampton and crossed the Bay of Biscay off the coast of France. Immediately, we found ourselves in the grip of a Force 8 gale. The ship was tossed and thrown about like a toy in a bathtub. We were all so ill that we were confined to our cabin for the first three days of the journey. It was not until we'd passed the Rock of Gibraltar that we were able to emerge to explore our new surroundings. However, when we headed to the restaurant for our first meal, the food was totally inappropriate for children and included rich Italian tortes laced with copious quantities of alcohol. So we lived on packets of potato crisps and cans of Pepsi for most of the journey.

We sailed on through the Mediterranean. For my pedantic father, it was extremely important that we could spell the name of this most difficult of seas. Many times during our voyage, he would suddenly ask, 'And how do you spell Mediterranean?' My brother Jeffrey and I, who were born eleven months apart, causing us to be mistaken for twins, would need to have it trip off the end of our tongues, letter perfect.

Whilst the ship had left the United Kingdom, it was not only Britons who were making the move to Australia. Our first Italian port of call was Genoa, followed by Naples, and then Messina on the island of Sicily. At each of those locations, there were hundreds of people waiting on the shore to embark on our ship. Many of the women were dressed in black, farewelling relatives who were leaving the country or getting on the ship themselves. The enormity of the upheaval of these moves to foreign lands was echoed in the heartfelt wailing of these families, both from the docks and on board the ship. They howled as though their hearts were breaking—deep primal cries of mothers who might never see their children again. These scenes were nothing like the streamer-laden images we so often see of departing passengers on a pleasure cruise.

We sailed on, across the top of Africa and anchored off the coast of Port Said at the northern end of the Suez Canal, waiting for permission to head down this narrow access route to the Indian Ocean. Small boats would come out to the ship, laden with wares to sell to the ship's passengers. Even though he did not smoke, my father bought a cigarette case inlaid with mother-of-pearl. It was common practice for passengers to purchase these goods and seemed to be expected to boost the local economy.

As we passed through the canal, we ran across the top deck, from port to starboard, surprised at how close we were to the land on either side.

We berthed in the port of Djibouti at the southern end of the canal. We were supposed to stop in Aden, but we were told that there was 'fighting' in that city and the ship was forbidden from docking there. The Aden Emergency had been in force since 1963, with the pro-Egyptian forces of the National Liberation Front attempting to oust the British who had controlled the territories of South Arabia since 1839. By November of 1967, the British had left, and the independent People's Republic of South Yemen was formed. But for a moment, I got to live that history in real time.

Tensions were also mounting between Israel and the Arab states, and within three months, the Suez Canal would be closed to international sea traffic. Future emigres would travel to Australia via the Cape of Good Hope at the southernmost tip of Africa.

Of course, as an eight-year-old, I was unaware of the scale of these hostilities, but it was evident that the adults were most concerned and spoke in small groups out of earshot of young children. For me, it just added another layer of excitement to our extraordinary adventure.

We continued to sail into the Indian Ocean. As we passed over the equator, it was a signal for Crossing ceremonies, a tradition for all ships which passed this imaginary line in the water. There were festivities around the pool which included a crew member dressed as Neptune, complete with long white beard and trident. We were all required to be 'baptised' in the swimming pool. It was a fun, chaotic event on a very hot day.

For a period of time, the lifts on the ship were broken—soda drink cans had been stuffed into the mechanism, so we had to use the stairwells for all movement around the ship.

When the Italian mothers began washing their children's cloth nappies in the swimming pool, that oasis of coolness became out of bounds to us.

As the ship was an Italian liner, all announcements, verbal and written, were in Italian. Given the number of English immigrants, it caused communication problems for the entire trip. We were never quite sure what, if any, actions were required of us as we arrived at each port. My parents struggled to ensure they had all the necessary information to leave the ship and return in time for the next departure. This new language also added to the foreignness of the experience and reinforced the move far away from all that was familiar and understandable.

We arrived in Fremantle as our first port of call in Australia. Many passengers disembarked here, and we said farewell to a number of friends we had made on the crossing. We sailed on to Melbourne where we disembarked. Finally our aquatic adventure was over.

We were taken to the Hotel Windsor in Spring Street where we stayed for a week while our house in Bendigo was being finished. Despite the hotel being very posh, dad ordered six glasses of milk in the restaurant because we had spent the past five weeks drinking powdered milk on the ship. This caused the bewildered restaurant manager to raise his eyebrows.

We would race up and down the stairs, trying to beat the lift, which was very old fashioned and had gilded, cage-like doors. Our antics were frowned upon and caused much tut-tutting from guests and staff because the Windsor was principally a hotel for adults.

On our arrival, it happened to be St Patrick's day, and there was a parade in Spring Street. We wondered if this was how all immigrants from the UK were greeted on their first day in the country.

And then, the hotel adventure was over. At the end of the week, we moved to Bendigo to begin our new Australian lives.

At sea, my dreams had been filled with the sights and sounds of each day's adventure. I was full of excitement and anticipation of the life that awaited us. In those confines of that cabin, surrounded by family from floor to ceiling, The Darkness was nowhere to be seen. It had disappeared.

I hoped the bright sunlight of our new homeland would keep him hidden.
Wishful thinking indeed.

THE CHAIR

Magpie warblings filled the air on our first autumn days in our new Bendigo home, a sound so new and unfamiliar to our British ears. There was much that was unlike the world we had left behind—bright blue skies rather than the grey smog of the Sheffield steelworks, the sense of space and openness, the brown landscape of rainless months, and the striking gray and silver of the gum trees.

I went to the local primary school, Flora Hill—where I proved to be a novelty to the rest of my Grade 3 classmates. I would find myself surrounded in the playground, with an older boy encouraging others to gather round.

'Go on,' he'd insist. 'Go on. Say something in English.' I was initially taken aback by this request, especially as this was my native tongue and that was the language we were all speaking. I came to realise that he wanted to hear me speak, to hear me say anything so that he and others could hear my broad Yorkshire accent.

I didn't mind this temporary time in the spotlight, and given my capacity to mimic the accents of those around me, it was not long before I had joined the throng and became Australianised—retaining, still to this day, just the faintest traces of my British accent.

It was around this time that I became an avid reader, with the school and city libraries proving to be treasure troves for my adventures into the fictional worlds that I so loved. And my favourite by far was Enid Blyton. She created wonderful worlds in which the children were in charge and had the most fun when the adults were not around. In fact, grown-ups were often bad people, doing the wrong things and needing their faults to be uncovered and rectified by the Famous Five, the Secret Seven or the Find-Outers.

The themes in her books were about being good and doing the right thing, taking care of friends and siblings, and especially having fun and going on picnics to eat boiled eggs and drink lashings of ginger beer.

But without a doubt, my favourite theme was that of secrets. And Enid Blyton's books were always full of secrets.

The children always knew the secret, but most importantly, the adults did not.

The Boy Next Door tells the story of Kit, who arrives at the big empty house late one night and is discovered by the children who live next door. It is all so mysterious—why is he not allowed to play in the garden? Why do the grown-ups deny his presence? Who are the strange men in the village searching for this boy? The children keep Kit safe and out of sight of the 'bad' men.

In the end, the children are victorious. They hide Kit in a place that only they know. The bad men who want to kidnap Kit because he is heir to his missing father's millions, are rounded up by the police. And thrillingly, Kit's not-really-missing father suddenly appears, rescues him; and they all live, literally, happily ever after.

This was my favourite Enid Blyton story. The children had a secret which they never divulged, and this kept Kit safe until he was rescued by his father.

Secrets could be a good thing. Secrets could keep people safe.

It arrived under the cover of darkness. Under the covers. In the dark.

I was young—very young—when it entered my life. We met but were never formally introduced. We got to know each other well. It was ever-present. But to others, it was invisible. And it was always silent. The silence was paramount.

It sat on my shoulder and whispered in my ear, 'I am here. I will always be here. Forever. You can never forget about me. But remember, you can tell no one. Ever. It is our secret. I am your Secret.'

I was afraid of its menace, its power to intimidate. I wanted it to feel reassured, to know that it had nothing to fear.

'I know that. You do not have to remind me. I will

ACT 2 — THE CHAIR

not forget. I promised. I am a good girl. I keep my promises. For ever and ever.'

On rare occasions, it would leave my shoulder and sit in the corner of the room. Whatever room I was in. It still felt oppressive, but I could breathe a little easier, a little more deeply. But it was ever-present, and I felt its vigilance.

We kept an unhealthy distance from one another. I became reconciled to its unwavering presence. We found a balance in our relationship. We each knew our place, the role we had to play.

The house was eerily quiet on that autumn day in 1967, without the usual sounds of a bustling family life. For some reason, long forgotten, I was alone—alone with him. In daylight. With no one else in the house.

As the sun streamed through the windows, the carpet began to smell as only sunlight can make it smell—musty and overpowering.

I do not recall how The Chair appeared in the lounge room. It seemed to rise out of the floor. It was a straight back chair. It did not belong here. It belonged with the other chairs, around the dining table—a perfect set of six. For the perfect family of six.

Suddenly, The Chair was beckoning to me. I was pulled in by my curiosity and found myself in its strange and welcoming embrace. I sat straddle-legged on its seat. I knew what would happen next—it had happened before.

But not in daylight—not like this, in the middle of the day, in the middle of the family home. The sunlight was almost more jarring and unsettling than the act itself. Where were the shadows? Where was the safety of the covers of my bed? At least then, it was hidden, just as a secret should be hidden. This was out in the open, and it was even more terrifying. What if anyone came home? Did it want us to be caught? Being found out was not an option. Then, The Secret would be out. And I was so proud of my nine-year-old self. I had told no-one; I had kept The Secret.

Today, it didn't seem to care. Had it no respect for The Secret?

Then it was over, and I scurried away to my bedroom, my heart racing and my hands shaking. I lay on my bed and watched the ceiling spin around and around. Eventually, it slowed down, and I cautiously sat up, listening for any sounds.

It was okay. The house was still empty. We had not been seen. The Secret was safe.

THE DRESSING GOWN

'Quiet, children. Quiet. It is almost time. Bring your seats to the front of the classroom and make sure you can see the television.'

We all did as we were told, pushing one another out of the way, hoping to get the best view. It was a very big day. We had been building up to this moment for weeks, and now it was here. We had a television in our Grade 5 classroom.

After a year or so of living in Bendigo, my father was not happy with his employment status at the hospital. He believed that he was not undertaking the role he had been promised as part of his contract and the reason we had come to Australia.

He had discovered that a classmate from his university days was operating a private practice in Terrigal, about an hour's drive north of Sydney. Ian was looking for a doctor to join him, to help lighten his workload. After exploring this little beachside town with its scenic ocean views and its warmer climate, he decided we would relocate.

Being a beach bunny was a favourite pastime, and I soon developed a deep tan. This lifestyle felt more like the Australia we had imagined rather than the dryness of central Victoria.

And it was here, at Terrigal Primary School, that we were watching the small black-and-white portable TV set perched on the teacher's desk. She had already turned it on so it could warm up as we settled into our viewing spots. The picture was grainy and the images hard to see. Mrs Marsden adjusted the 'rabbit ears,' which acted as the aerial on top of the box. It didn't make any difference. A number of other teachers appeared and stood behind our semicircle of chairs. We leaned in and a hush descended over the room.

We were able to see the legs of the space craft, planted on the moon's surface. It was time for the first moon walk. Suddenly, a man spoke in a slow American drawl.

'We are seeing Neil Armstrong going down the ladder of the landing module.' He paused. 'He is now at the foot of the ladder.'

We heard the astronaut say, 'The surface of the moon is like a fine powder.'

And then he was standing on the moon. He was standing on the moon! We all clapped and cheered so loudly that we missed hearing those historical words, 'That's one small step for a man, one giant leap for mankind.'

The teachers shook hands and slapped each other on the back.

Humans had walked on a land far from earth. We were space travelers, and suddenly, the world seemed full of change and possibilities. It was the stuff of comic books, and it meant that my favourite TV shows, like *Doctor Who* in his Tardis, *Lost in Space* with the handsome Major West, *Star Trek* and *Thunderbirds*, took on a whole new realm of possibilities.

I loved to escape into the other worlds I found on the screen—interplanetary travel, worlds so very far removed from our own. This desire to escape, to act, to find any place or role that was as far removed as possible from the reality of my life has continued to this day.

This was a Monday to remember, and not just for the world event that we had witnessed.

'What's going on in there? What are you two doing?' My nine-year-old brother Jeffrey's voice broke the silence of the night as he lay in bed in the adjacent bedroom.

'We're just talking. Go back to sleep.' The Dressing Gown's voice was calm but determined.

I lay in the bed, unable to move or breathe. We formed a frozen tableau—the gown and me. Why had my brother woken up? He should have been asleep. He had gone to bed hours ago. He had never woken up before, or had he?

It was the house's fault. It was old, and my bedroom could only be accessed through Jeffrey's room. This design quirk had never caused any problems. Until tonight.

'Go back to sleep. Please please please go back to

sleep.' I silently willed him a lullaby to hasten his slumber, as much for his sake as for mine. This was my burden, my responsibility. It was something he did not need to know about. If I kept The Secret, I could keep everyone safe.

As silence descended, the tableau defrosted, and the ritual continued. Dressing Gown, as always, was stifling hot and scratchy. I felt the loosened cord against my leg; and soon, Dressing Gown was on top of me, spreading my legs with one of its furry arms. I closed my eyes tightly and waited. Soon, the gown would rise and fall over my body, in time with my beating heart. Its breath would get heavier and faster; but it would stay quiet, so very, very quiet. Then it was out of the bed, regathered and retied. I was left in its musty wake as it wafted past the sleeping child and returned to the main house.

Jeffrey's intervention had been close—too close. Not since The Chair in the dining room had I felt so scared that The Secret would be discovered. I lay back down on the bed and closed my eyes. The Secret would be safe for another day.

When I was thirteen, I was a little taller than my friends at school and a bit pudgier.

'Now stand on the knot and use your arms to pull yourself up the rope. Touch the roof and come down again. Up!'

And up they would go. All the fit, bright young girls, keen to please the gym teacher. Miss Carruthers was a cliché, cut from gym-teacher cloth—long blond hair, neat athletic figure and a tan that showed she lived an outdoors life. She padded lightly across the school yard like a panther. Boys, too young to understand why, would turn their heads to watch her pass. Years later, she married the male cliché gym teacher—a combination that surely produced genetically perfect children, for whom rope climbing would literally be in their DNA.

But I just stood on the knot and swung backwards and forwards, backwards and forwards—like a human version of the ticking, clicking, monotonous metronome I endured in my piano lessons. I never did achieve the *up*, not once. In front of all those nimble, monkey-like climbers, I was alone with my inadequacy. As I looked around at my classmates, I had an increasing sense that I was different.

And this difference had only a little to do with my inability to climb ropes.

THE KARATE KID

In 1972, my father had found the working hours at the practice in Terrigal to be far longer and more arduous than he had imagined. As he was beginning to explore new work opportunities, the hospital in Bendigo, which we had left in 1968, was able to offer him the role for which he had been originally contracted.

So we moved away from the coast and back to Bendigo. Of course, this meant that we started school all over again that year, in a different state school system, with new teachers and had to make new friends.

We had experienced three significant moves in less than five years.

This ongoing dislocation and disconnection from all that was familiar meant that the only constant element was the family—reinforcing it as the focus and hub of our lives.

I joined a dojo and began to learn karate.

A hush came over the all-male crowd as they moved to form a circle around the unusual objects placed in the middle of the church hall. Their rampant expectations hovered above the silence.

As I approached the outer edge of this human wreath, the onlookers parted and allowed me to enter. I fumbled with my belt, newly dyed to a deep green, straightened my white tunic top and tried to steady my breath. This was not a friendly crowd. I was sure they were hoping to see me fail. The fifteen-year-old gladiator was entering the arena, and they were all waiting to give the thumbs-down signal.

I neared the centrepiece—two columns of housing bricks which held a single roofing tile between them, four feet off the floor. I had only one task—to break that tile with my bare hand. I had been building up to this moment for months, and now the time was here. The encroaching crowd and my stubborn pride would not allow me to turn back.

I scanned the room, feigning an air of confidence, and adopted the necessary stance. With my left leg forward and right leg back, I lifted my right arm over my head, gently lowered my hand and tapped the top of the tile. I did this several times, adding drama and tension to the moment. Beads of sweat dropped on the tile's surface. The crowd edged closer; the circle tightened around me. I was enveloped in a fog of beer-laden breaths, as the breathing grew more rapid, matching my own.

The time for stalling was over. I took a sharp intake of breath, focused my gaze on the target and visualised my hand passing through it. I lifted my arm once more, tensed all the muscles in my hand and brought its full force down onto that tile. There was a loud cracking noise. No-one was more amazed than me to see that it had shattered into several dozen pieces and lay on the floor.

I had done it.

Despite my elation, I displayed a cool indifference. I stood tall, rearranged my tunic and strode calmly out of the circle, to a smattering of grudgingly respectful applause. I sensed their disappointment at my success.

I moved away from the throng, walked out of the hall and into the fresh night air. Out of sight, I was able to do what I could not inside. I grabbed my right hand with my left, squeezed them both tight and lowered my head between my knees.

I was in agony. It really hurt. A lot.

In all the build-up to this event, no-one had warned me that breaking the tile would hurt so much. It was just as well because that ignorance helped get me through. *Thank God it was over.*

My dojo had offered to put on this karate display for the local lads of Castlemaine, forty kilometres from Bendigo, which was only a ten-minute drive from the tiny country town of Faraday. The catalyst for this was an event in October 1972 in which two men had entered the one-teacher Faraday school and had kidnapped Ms Gibbs and all six of her pupils. They had been shoved into a van, and the kidnappers had demanded a million-dollar ransom from the Victorian government. During the night, the teacher had kicked her way out of the vehicle and escaped with the children.

The kidnappers were soon caught. It was a huge news story at the time and the focus of much conversation at our home. Unknown to me at the time, my parents had been discussing whether I should undertake training in deportment or self-defense classes. This episode tipped the balance and off to karate I was sent. (The subject of my deportment was never raised again. I've either gathered some along the way, or I have lived a 'deport-less' life.)

I signed up at the local karate club in early 1973 and was joined by a few of my school friends. Our young female presence was a novelty to the older male participants. I was not known for my physicality, so I was surprised that I took to it like a seasoned samurai warrior. We were students of Kyokushin—a new Japanese martial art formed in the mid 1960s.

It was a full contact style of karate, which meant that as we became more experienced, we sparred against one another, including the men in the group. After one particularly grueling fight with a much older, taller and heavier opponent, I was left with a bloodied nose and stars and twittering birds flying around my head, like a Looney Tunes cartoon. As I stumbled into the car at the end of training, it was a case of 'Yippity, yippity. That'll be all, folks.' But only for that night. I was soon back for more.

This had led to my participation in the display in Castlemaine as a fully fit, lethal fighting machine despite now nursing the sorest of hands. I had become a girl completely capable of defending myself in any situation in which I felt unsafe.

And yet when I was faced with the most threatening of situations, none of these instincts were evoked. For seven years, I had not employed a single kick, punch or other defensive move. No noses were bloodied. For some reason, I was unable to connect the dots, to appreciate that I was in danger. That false sense of security proved to be the greatest danger of all.

14
THE TORCH

'And the winner of the Academy Award for Best Picture is ... *The Sting*.'

We had already fallen in love with Robert Redford and Paul Newman in *Butch Cassidy and the Sundance Kid*, and here they were again, just as handsome and daring as ever. Scott Joplin's catchy piece of music, 'The Entertainer,' brought back the era of ragtime; and pianists all over the world, including those in our house, were buying the sheet music and practicing furiously.

In contrast to this movie about conmen, deceit and lies, I was playing Lady Alice More in a production of *A Man for All Seasons* about Sir Thomas More who, as Lord Chancellor, would not support King Henry VIII's desire to divorce Catherine of Aragon so that he could marry Anne Boleyn. It was a play about conscience and standing up for one's beliefs and truths, regardless of the cost. Alice does not understand her husband's decision. Surely, it is easier to give the king what he wants? Must he die for his principles? By the end of the play, she accepts his decision, trusting that God will provide him with the answers which have so eluded her.

I enjoyed this role. I was never happier than when I was on stage. You could give me a script, tell me what you wanted from the character, and I could deliver. I loved inhabiting another being and stepping out of my real life.

One afternoon, the director sat us all down after rehearsal.

'I really want you to understand the enormity of this play's message—how being true to yourself and your beliefs can have extraordinary consequences. Would you be prepared to risk everything—for a principle?'

This was a big question and it unsettled me. What did this mean for me? Was I living a principled life? Was I being true to myself? No matter the cost?

This introspection seemed like a lot of hard work. Besides, Sir Thomas lost his head for sticking to his beliefs, which was surely the direst of all consequences. If he had just kept quiet, his life would have been spared. In my mind, that seemed like the preferred option.

I decided I did not like asking myself these questions. They were too confronting. In that moment, I made the choice to stop thinking about whether I was living an authentic life.

Instead, I continued my crush on Dylan Adamson, my husband in the play—my Man for All Seasons.

That was so much easier.

ACT 2 — THE TORCH

The bedroom door opened, and a circle of light darted across the ceiling above my head like a searchlight scanning the night sky. During World War II, such lights were used to defend cities against enemy bombing raids. The arrival of The Torch felt like an omen—no-one would be coming to my defense.

The door closed, and The Torch tiptoed across the room and settled by my bedside. The flickering flashlight had become a regular visitor. I would soon be caught in its insidious beam.

To my shame and bewilderment, on more than one occasion, I found myself waiting expectantly for its arrival. Sometimes, the sensations I experienced as The Torch shone over and then into my body were warming and pleasant. I'd feel a burst of light in my head and body, like a fireworks finale, exploding and exploding, before they faded away across a night sky. The Torch's own euphoric reaction made me feel wanted and special.

But at other times, I wished The Torch had never appeared and had stayed in its place in the bottom drawer of the kitchen. I was beginning to feel a growing disquiet, that this was wrong, not normal, not how other fathers and daughters behaved. But what could I do? So I lay still, did not struggle. It was better this way. For everyone.

I fervently believed that by keeping The Secret, I was safeguarding my family's integrity and unity. I was responsible for everyone's security. If I angered The Secret, allowed this hideous arachnid to move down its web, away from its hiding spot, I would bring disaster and shame, not only to myself but to the whole family.

So I made a vow that I would never breach the sanctity of The Secret.

As I grew older, I learned I had the power to extinguish The Torch. With determined shallow breathing and by keeping my eyes closed (but not too tight) despite the warm glare of its incandescent bulb, I became the master of this unmoving pose. Breath slow and steady. Eyes wide shut. And hold. Hold. Hold. Repeat. The Torch had to believe that I was deep, deep asleep.

When I got it just right, there was a click, and the room returned to its darkened state. As time passed, I learned that it ceased to shine if it sensed its presence was unwelcome. And so The Torch would shuffle across the room and leave as noiselessly as it entered.

I had silenced the air raid siren. The townsfolk were safe for the night.

15
LEAVING HOME

As the Chief sent the cart crashing through the window of the asylum and made his break for freedom, there was a smattering of applause from the audience and a couple of cheers from the back row in the movie theatre. We were all caught up in the moment and so thrilled that someone had escaped the clutches of the Cuckoo's Nest. We had hoped it would be Jack Nicholson, but once he'd had his lobotomy, we knew that the likelihood of his escape was lost.

I sat in silence as the credits rolled up the screen. I had never seen a movie like this. It was raw and confronting, and the lines between the good and bad guys were unclear. The white hats and black hats had become grey.

As my best friend Tom and I left the theatre, it took time before I found words to make conversation about what we had just seen. He too seemed stunned into unusual silence because he was the most worldly person I knew. I mean, he had introduced me to Stone's Green Ginger Wine and Indonesian clove cigarettes.

We were in the final weeks of high school, and I was working hard to ensure I got the results I needed to get into university. But I was finding it difficult to focus. There were so many distractions—even the fact that we didn't have to wear uniforms to school meant that every morning I was rifling through my wardrobe to find clothes that suggested I was in with the cool crowd. An oversized jumper, worn with those new salmon-coloured jeans that zipped up the back, combined with desert boots, was my favourite look. If only I could have worn that five days a week.

As well as studying, I was rehearsing for the school play, *Roots* by Arnold Wesker. Once again, Dylan Adamson and I were playing the lead roles; and once again, my crush was in full swing.

I was involved with the debating team, the madrigal singing group and was working at Woolies every Friday night and Saturday morning.

I was finishing my school days with a bang.

A fire actually. The sixth form students had been given the use of a common room, with ancient sofas, mattresses and cushions. We listened to the Rolling Stones, took great pride in missing classes and believed we were completely anti-establishment.

One night, the common room burnt to the ground. A burning cigarette butt had likely been left on one of the couches. We didn't feel quite so cool after we lost our hangout.

We donned our uniforms for the final day, shredding our skirts so we looked like hula dancers.

Then we headed to the local lake and took turns

ACT 2 — LEAVING HOME

throwing one another in the water. It was as though we were washing away twelve years of chalk and ink.

University was the next step for me. I was keen to move out of home and claim the freedom I needed in so many ways.

I had kept The Secret safe. I hadn't breached the covenant and was sure it had never been discovered by others. I wanted to leave it at home and not take it with me to my new life and into my new beginning. It was intact at home, surrounded by the impenetrable walls of its own strongbox.

At least if it was with me, I knew where it was—at all times. I had always known that The Secret needed to be kept—forever. I wondered if that meant it had to be kept *with me* forever?

We had spent so much time together. A part of me couldn't imagine life without it. I knew what it took to keep it where it belonged. And by this stage, it didn't take up all that much room. Might as well throw it in for the trip with the rest of my belongings.

So on a bright sunny day in February 1977, at the age of eighteen, and with my second-hand Fiat 850 Coupe filled to the brim with all my earthly possessions, I headed down the highway to Melbourne, with my parents following behind in their car.

We pulled up in front of Sugden Tower, Queen's College at the University of Melbourne, along with all the other freshmen and their parents.

As I looked around, my excitement was tempered by a glaring reality—I was the only person in a gaudy multi-coloured dress, handmade by her mother. I was mortified. I had not wanted to hurt my mother's feelings, so I wore the dress she had so lovingly created. But in that moment, it made me feel I was different from everyone else once again. I was self-conscious that even though this was a new beginning in a city far from home, I was not like any of the other young women.

Why couldn't I just fit in? Just be like everyone else? For once in my life.

After we had unpacked the contents of the cars into my tiny ground-floor room, it was time for mum and dad to leave. After I waved them goodbye, I sat on the edge of my bed and cried until dinner time. I was not yet homesick, so why was I crying? This was what I wanted—my own place, away from home, with lots of like-minded, nervous-but-excited freshers.

I gathered myself together and headed to the communal bathroom to wash my face.

Then it dawned on me—these were tears of bliss, sheer joy at being away from home.

I had finally moved far away from The Darkness, The Chair, The Dressing Gown and The Torch. They were all behind me.

There was just one more chasm to cross.

THE CONVERSATION

We sat, side by side, on the single bed in my college room. I was nineteen years old and in my second year at university.

And I was about to have a conversation with my father that no daughter should ever need to have.

If anyone knew what I was about to say to him, it would make no sense. But it was a necessary discussion.

I was conscious I had difficult news for him. The most monumental of events had occurred in my life, and he needed to be informed. I had told no-one else. But he needed to know—right then and there. I was agonizing because I did not want to hurt his feelings. *His* feelings?

'Dad, I have something to tell you, and I want you to just listen and not say anything until I have finished.' I knew it was going to be difficult enough, so I needed to be able to speak without interruptions.

His eyebrows raised, and he pursed his lips. He was not used to being spoken to in this way. When we were growing up, it was the children in our family who listened to our father.

His style had always been dominating, and he would tolerate no challenge to his authority.

'Dad, I have met someone. A really special man and... hmm... he is a soldier, an officer in the army.' This had nothing to do with the news I was about to impart, but for some reason, I thought this man's career choice might make it all the more acceptable.

Before he could speak, I added, 'And we love each other, very much, and so, the other night we, er, had sex. I am telling you that I am no longer a virgin.'

Given all that had happened in our past, this may seem like a ludicrous pronouncement. But as far as I was concerned, I had been a virgin.

As a young girl, I'd always believed that a woman's virginity was hers to give. She should choose the most perfect of circumstances and proffer this most intimate of gifts to the person she decided was worthy to receive it. But to cope with the years of abuse, I had created a distinction between what had happened between me and my father and all subsequent relationships.

So when it came time to have consensual sex for the first time, as far as I was concerned, I was a virgin. I was entitled to begin my sex life afresh, with a metaphorically intact hymen. That may have been a physical impossibility but not a psychological one. I was complete, whole, pure, unspoiled, and was able to present my virginal self to the man of my choosing.

I looked expectantly at my father, trying to regulate my anxious breathing. What would he say? What *could* he say?

Finally, 'I knew this day would come,' he said, his shoulders slumped and his eyes downcast. 'It was just a matter of time.'

He paused and then added, 'And you needed to find the right man.'

I wanted to say, 'Yes, because you have always been the wrong man,' but instead, I said, 'He is very special and we love each other very much.'

And so it was done.

You might say this was a break-up.

This was nonsense, of course. There was no correlation between our sexual past and my new, 'virginal' relationship. But for some reason, I knew this milestone would make it easier for him to accept the formal end of his abuse.

He'd been unable to abuse me for the past two years while I was at university, but he'd continued to behave inappropriately towards me. Whenever he saw me, he would hold me very close—too close—for far too long. As he held me, he would smell my hair, smooth it with his hands and make comments about his love for me.

But as usual, I had done nothing to stop these behaviours. Why hadn't I taken a firmer stand, defended myself and forged a new paradigm for us? Why did I continue to see him, when I lived a hundred kilometres from home and could have refused to have any contact? Why did I continue to keep The Secret?

I knew the reason. The all-encompassing, ever-present reason.

The family did not know. It was still our secret. I had continued to play the role of a dutiful daughter, and if that changed, family members would ask questions I did not want to answer. I was still keeping my part of the bargain—I was going to keep this secret regardless of the cost to me. I had never known a time without The Secret and couldn't see any point in hurting the family at this late stage. I could continue to hold out, and by my silence, ensure the family remained safe.

As far as The Secret was concerned, nothing had changed. It was still in its rightful hidden place.

The sanctity of The Secret was further reinforced when my father said, 'Now when people go into a serious relationship, when they have met the person they want to spend the rest of their life with, they usually tell each other everything about their past, like previous boyfriends and lovers.'

He paused, stared deep into my eyes and enunciated very clearly, 'This is not one of those things.'

To anyone else, this directive may have seemed outlandish, nonsensical—surely, there should be no secrets from your future life partner. But I knew exactly what he meant—I knew all too well how *this* was to be treated.

I simply nodded. No further explanation or discussion was required. The Secret was meant to be kept—forever.

I had no problem with this directive. I planned to keep The Secret in its locked box and throw away the key. There was no need for it to ever see the light of day.

This sanctity of The Secret was so ingrained that I shared it with no-one, including the man who, less than three years later, would become my husband.

The chat was over. I was pleased with my newfound courage and determination to take a stand in asserting my independence. I was finally changing the relationship between me and my father.

To the outside world, we had always had a 'normal' father and daughter relationship.

For me, this day marked a new beginning.

I felt like an adult for the first time in my life.

From here on in, I would make my own decisions and live the life I chose for myself.

On that day, I took the first steps.

ACT 3
FLASHFORWARD

THE UNRAVELLING

We had been driving for hours, along the highway, in a convoy of two. I made sure I kept sight of his car in front, on occasion speeding up as it disappeared around a curve in the road.

The dry brown paddocks stretched for miles on either side of the road, and the other traffic was intermittent. An occasional tractor would slow our pace, but we had been making good time on this significant journey to a new state and a new life.

I had been thinking about what lay ahead for us when the car in front pulled over to the side of the road. Why was he stopping here? We still had a long way to go, and there was no evidence of the town which we had agreed would be the next place to refuel the cars and ourselves.

I pulled in behind him. He was out of his car and heading towards a sign on the side of the road. I followed, eager to understand the reason for this unexpected delay.

'Welcome to Queensland,' it read. We had reached the border.

He walked towards me, took me in his arms and said, pointing at the sign, 'Welcome to Queensland. Thanks for making this big move, for changing everything in your life and coming with me. You are the bravest person I know. I love you so much.'

I began to cry as the emotions of the past few weeks found an outlet, pushing myself further into his warm embrace.

'I love you too, and this is where I am meant to be. With you. Wherever you are, that's our new home.'

He kissed me on the forehead, and we headed back to our cars. We were soon in automobile lockstep, continuing to our destination, Brisbane.

It was Easter 1983, I was twenty-four years old, and John and I had been engaged for five months.

We had met in December 1980, at the Puckapunyal army camp in the middle of Victoria. I was twenty-two years old, a corporal in the Army Reserve, earning my university spending money as a drill instructor for the sixteen-day recruit courses. He was a regular army sergeant, a few years older than me and a veteran of Vietnam. He had been posted for two years to 'Pucka' to support the army reserve in its huge expansion during this time. He was so much younger and more handsome than the sergeants I knew in the reserve, who were often retired from the regular army after many years of service, some of them veterans of the Korean War.

I have always said that our eyes met across a crowded parade ground. Following that meeting, we reconnected in January 1981 for another training course, and I decided that he was a man definitely worth pursuing. We had our first date on Valentine's Day, which just happened to be the next Saturday night that we could both get together. Our relationship flourished over the next two years, so when he had asked what I wanted for my birthday at the end of 1982, I had replied, 'An engagement ring.'

Now it was time for him to take up his new posting at the army base in Enoggera.

A Queenslander through and through, he was passionate about his state and especially Brisbane, where he was born and raised. He was going home.

The long hours behind the wheel gave me much time for contemplation, daydreaming and remembering. He was right—this was a big step for me. I had left school six years earlier, attended university in Melbourne and been living in Fitzroy for the past two years—all just a hundred and fifty kilometres from my parents' home.

When I received my university offers at the end of 1976, I had two options—study a double degree in Arts and Law at the Australian National University or undertake a Bachelor of Arts at the University of Melbourne. It was my first fork in the road—if I had gone to Canberra, I might have become a solicitor, or perhaps a barrister, given my love of acting. But at the time, I wanted to stay close enough to be able to see my siblings on a regular basis—the pull of our close-knit family was greater than my legal ambitions and that, combined with success in my humanities subjects at school, the decision to go to Melbourne felt like it offered the right balance of distance and closeness.

I had returned home frequently during my university years and was also an avid letter writer. In return, I would receive letters from my parents and siblings. We still displayed all the trappings of a 'normal' family—and it was my responsibility to keep it just that way for as long as possible.

One day in 1986, quite unexpectedly, without warning, The Secret moved. It left my shoulder, where it had sat for so long. And more surprisingly, it never ever spent any time in the corner. It began to sit over my heart, crushing it, causing it to beat faster and erratically. Then it filled the pit of my stomach and began gnawing at my innards, like a trapped rodent, consuming me from the inside. It filled my head, my daylight hours and my horror-filled nights.

The Secret was taking over my life. I no longer felt as if I had any control over it anymore.

John and I had been married for almost three years, and our lives were well and truly established in Brisbane. We had bought a home which was walking distance from John's unit on the army base. I was working as the personnel officer at the Pick n Pay Hypermarket at Aspley—a new concept in shopping which had controversially opened in 1984. With its vast array of goods, it was the first store combining the products of a department store with those of a supermarket, and its size was such that it could incorporate a line of seventy-five checkouts.

It had been initiated by a South African company, and the unions had picketed the building of this massive enterprise in protest at the apartheid regime of that country. Of course, Joh Bjelke-Petersen, the premier of Queensland, was unmoved by their actions. He was an avid supporter of developers, so the building was completed, and the opening had been accompanied by much fanfare. Flo, Joh's wife, had been the first customer through the checkouts.

We were living a cocooned, sheltered life in a state of conservatism designed to keep us feeling safe, unaffected by the larger national issues. We were constantly being reassured by our leader's favourite instruction to his constituents, 'Don't you worry about that.'

I may have been reassured, externally. But internally, I was experiencing a growing sense of unease. The unsettling had been creeping up on me for some months. It was as though pieces were starting to fall from my exterior, like paint from an aging weatherboard house, exposing an uncovered surface in need of repair.

It became all-consuming, and I could think of nothing else. I was not sleeping. I wanted to resign from my job and run away even though I had no idea where I would run to, or indeed, why I was running.

I knew that something was very wrong for me and that I needed help. What had happened to trigger these unsettled and confused feelings in me?

For the first time in my memory, that topic of sexual

abuse, in all its forms, was being openly discussed. Articles appeared in papers, magazines and thanks to Oprah Wifrey, who announced that she had been sexually abused as a nine-year-old by a relative, it became the subject of discussion on daytime television. I felt overwhelmed by the exposure and the lack of secrecy. Why couldn't people just leave it alone? Leave it buried where it belonged? I didn't want to be made to think about it, or have my world filled with other people's tawdry revelations. I had dealt with my past—why couldn't they deal with theirs?

Of course, none of this was true. The way I had dealt with my past was simply to set and forget. I had always known this was not a solution and that I'd expected a Band-Aid would be enough to cover the suppurating wound. But it had worked for so long—I must have used a particularly large and effective virtual Elastoplast.

But now the world was changing, and I felt as if my past was no longer my own. Just as my Secret and I were out of balance, so was the rest of the world. People were speaking about the unspeakable in forums and in greater numbers than ever before. A ground swell was gathering momentum, and I felt like Charlie Brown being caught up in the giant snowball that Lucy had sent down the hill for him.

I knew it was time to tell John about my past. We had been dating since 1981 and married since 1983, and I had never told him about my childhood abuse. Just as my father had reinforced on that day in 1978, I had told no-one. I was ashamed, embarrassed, and oddly, I didn't want John to think less of me—or bizarrely, my father. Why was that important to me? If dad was a bad person, what did that make me? I was an accomplice, complicit in the crime, and I did not want John's opinion of me to be sullied by the behaviours of the past.

I was a mess. I decided to get some professional help. I saw my doctor, told him I was having some 'problems' and he referred me to a psychology clinic. My embarrassment caused me to be vague about the underlying issues, so when I entered the room and saw I would be speaking to a man, I realised I should have been more specific.

I was uncomfortable from the moment I sat down. I am sure most men would be empathetic to the circumstances of my past and would deplore the abuse and be horrified at what my father had done to me. But in that moment, I couldn't get over the fact that it was a man who had done this to me. I couldn't relate to the therapist and did not go back to see him again.

However, he suggested I attend a group therapy session for women who had experienced childhood sexual abuse. I had no idea what I needed, so I went along to the meeting in a Department of Health building in Ipswich.

The room was full of chairs arranged in a circle, and women of all ages were arriving. After nervous glances around the room, each took a seat. A man started speaking (*Oh, great. The facilitator is a man*, I thought to myself. This was not a good start). After explaining that this was a group therapy session and that we were all encouraged to say as much or as little as made us feel comfortable, a woman began to speak.

'Sometimes, I worry that I am going to kill my partner in the night.'

She certainly had our full attention.

'Why is that?' asked the facilitator, straining to keep his voice calm.

'Well, sometimes I have nightmares and think that he is going to rape me. If I stab him and kill him, will I get off because I was abused as a child and I thought he was my abuser?'

The man was trying to be very calm, although I thought I saw beads of sweat forming on his brow.

'Yes, well, let's be very clear. If you kill your partner just because you thought he was your former abuser, that would be no defense. You would go to jail for murder.'

The girl shrugged, looked most disappointed and was not heard from again for the rest of the session. I sensed we were all wondering if she just wanted to use her childhood abuse as an excuse for getting away with murder—literally.

Another woman suddenly blurted out, 'I never want to get pregnant because I worry that I might have a boy, and I can't stand the thought of carrying a man inside me for all those months.' She ran sobbing from the room.

This session was not at all what I had expected.

I did not feel that I had anything to say to this group of strangers. I was contemplating my next move when another participant said, 'I'm here because I was touched inappropriately by an uncle when I was eleven-years-old.'

I found my mind reeling. Oh, for God's sake, you

were touched once—only *once*? Get over it. As the four Yorkshiremen in Monty Python would say, 'Luxury!' Where were the serially abused women? Where were my peers?

I began to wonder. Was there a hierarchy of abuse? Did people earn higher status in the world of the abused if it started at an earlier age, had been endured for a longer period of time, with a greater degree of frequency, and just for good measure, with full penetration? Part of me wanted to yell, 'Get some time up, people. You are not playing in the big leagues. My abuse is more worthy than yours. I have more abuse credibility.'

Even as I had these thoughts, I knew they were extremely unfair. Everyone's abuse is terrible and traumatic, and I had no right to belittle their suffering because of my own perceived pecking order.

I could have contributed more to the conversation as it went around the room. I could have spoken up to share that there was hope, that no-one needed to be defined by their abusive past, that they could fight off the lethargy and victim mentality and grab life by the throat.

But that was not my job. I was dealing with my own stuff, and each person there needed to deal with theirs.

I left that meeting, determined that things were not as bad as I had thought. I just needed to pull myself together and everything would be okay.

I could not have been more wrong.

SECRET NO MORE

I have a series of memories—distorted, jerky, unclear. Like an old celluloid movie coming to the last of its frames, slipping and sliding through the aperture. Like a dream you remember vividly as soon as you wake up but within moments, begins to fade and only fragments remain.

Those were the events of late 1986. I finally told John about the childhood abuse as we wandered through the army base beside our home. I do not remember exactly what I said to him. He was kind and loving and overwhelmed. He had held my father in high regard, as did so many others. His image was shattered, and he found my father's behaviour hard to comprehend.

I left my job at the Hypermarket—my restlessness had made my departure inevitable.

Not long after, for reasons long forgotten, I found myself travelling to Victoria with my parents after they came for a visit. The long car trip was hot and uncomfortable. Why was I heading into the lion's den, and why was the lion driving me there?

A few days later, my sister and I were sitting in a car outside the Bendigo Building Society as the rain cascaded down the windscreen. We hadn't seen each other for a while. The seven-year age difference between us was less of an issue now that we were older. Earlier, it had mattered. When I started high school, she was yet to start primary school. In the year that I headed off to university, she had just achieved double digits. She was my 'kid' sister, and we always seemed to have so little in common.

As the subject turned to our father, I bristled at his name. Thoughts of him had started to make me increasingly uncomfortable. I found that I didn't want to talk about him.

Clearly, I was not as subtle as I imagined because she turned to me and asked, 'Did you ever have problems with dad when you were younger?'

This question changed my life, the lives of everyone I loved, forever. It was an ending and a beginning in a single moment.

The years of silence and solitude, of secrets, of guilt and shame, welled up from a place so deep inside, from my very soul to my choking throat, into my startled staring eyes.

I felt the world brake—break—on its axis.

I spun towards her, my mind racing, my heart pounding.

Her question was the spark that reignited the smouldering fire inside me.

Of course, I knew what she meant. I knew precisely what she meant.

Oh my god, she knows. She knows! How can she know? I've told no-one. I've kept The Secret, faithfully, and now she knows...

As the enormity of her question seeped into my bewildered brain, I managed an almost imperceptible nod.

'Yes.'

The word was out there before I could stop it. The simplest of three-letter words. In that moment, I knew my life would never be the same again.

I burst into tears. Huge, gulping sobs that had been kept behind a fortress so strong that not a single drop of water could pass through its dense, thick walls. It was a lifetime of tears that had been waiting for their release. Sitting next to her, my defences were breached as the battering ram of her question broke through the ramparts.

As the tears fell and my fortress tumbled, a slurry of emotions was loosened. I was relieved that it was finally 'out there,' but I also felt disloyal to my father. I was a traitor—I'd betrayed The Secret.

It would be a long time before I could acknowledge that *his* betrayal had been the greatest of all. The man who was meant to be my greatest protector had used and abused my trust in the worst way of all.

At first, I struggled to comprehend the reason for my sister's question. I looked straight into her tear-filled eyes.

Then, at once, I was overcome with a dawning, sickening realisation—she had not known *my* secret.

She was not asking me because she'd discovered something I'd kept hidden.

She was asking because we shared the same terrible past.

'You too?' was all I could manage.

After an eternity, she nodded.

And my world crumbled.

Oh God, why was she nodding? Stop nodding. For pity's sake, stop nodding. It was not possible. I had kept The Secret so that no-one in the family would be hurt—I had been keeping everyone safe with my vow of silence. That had been my job for the past twenty years. It was the only thing that made sense during those tortuous years—I had been the saviour of our family.

But I had failed.

My whole life had been a lie. It had all been for nothing.

All that time, I had genuinely believed I was the chosen one, that I was special, and my silence had kept the family intact.

In that moment, I found out that when I left home, my little sister had lost her shield. She'd been unprotected, exposed to his depravity. He took up where we had left off—as though she was simply the next player in the batting line-up.

How could I have been so naïve, so unaware of this possibility?

Until that moment, it had never occurred to me that this could happen.

Not once.

I had always believed I was the special one. He had no need for another.

As I had grown up and away from our father, I imagined he would accept that this was a closed chapter. It was over. We would put the past in its strongbox, locked tight and bury it deep.

It would never need to be opened ever again.

For years I had been so relieved that it was in the past and that The Secret was safe. I had never exposed him. I had absolutely kept my part of the bargain. My reward was that our family remained whole and complete.

And now it was all a lie.

I wasn't special at all. I hadn't saved the family by keeping silent. In fact, the opposite was true. My silence had put my sister in harm's way. My silence had made me complicit in my sister's abuse.

I felt betrayed by my father all over again. How could this be happening to me? How much betrayal could one person endure?

But worst of all, I had betrayed my sister. My beautiful baby sister whom I had helped to feed and change when she was born, who was still playing with dolls while I was making my own way in the world. She did not deserve this.

I had dealt with my past. I had reconciled it within myself, had built a life in spite of it. This revelation blew it all up.

But beneath the obvious feelings lay other more complex emotions in that sludge of my feelings. Was it—could it be—jealousy? That she had been the new 'chosen one'? That she had been the bright, shiny new toy? *How dare he?*

I knew these thoughts were wrong and unfair and frankly, ludicrous as soon as they passed through the fogginess of my still-comprehending brain.

She had not sought to be abused. She certainly didn't feel special.

My sister continued to speak.

'Hmm… mum and I often wondered if you'd had trouble with dad too.'

What?

'What do you mean, "You and mum often wondered"? So mum knows about your abuse? When did you tell her? How long has she known?' I asked.

If she really had wondered, why had she never asked me? Was it because she (and my sister) had a 'saving the family' Secret too?

These were new revelations.

The icy crevice into which I was falling cracked further apart, wider and deeper. I was a trekker who had become untethered from the group. My ice pick was gone, and the crampons that had served me well for so long, which had held me fast on the slippery slopes of my life, were unbuckled and useless.

I was still trying to comprehend everything she'd told me, when she said, 'I think we should go and tell mum. We're due to meet her in half an hour anyway.'

Go and tell mum? Just like that? It all sounded so casual. Let's just pop over to the local hotel, order a glass of wine and then tell her The Secret that had been so long mine to keep. How could we?

I was in a fog. Now that The Secret was unleashed, I was ill-prepared for its exposure. I had been the keeper, the curator, the gravedigger of The Secret. I knew The Secret's every moment, from its very creation. I knew its nuances, its subtleties, how far it could be pushed, what it took to keep it silenced and where it was buried.

I knew that this was why it should never have been unearthed and needed to remain buried. When it was still a secret, it could take on all the hidden elements of something unseen, unspoken.

Now that it was exposed, it was real.

The next few days and months are hazy in my memory.

I sometimes wish I could remember what was said to whom, when and where. But I appreciate that my memory is trying to protect me from the past, as it had done so many times before.

I know the conversation with my mother was strained and awkward.

When I confronted my father, as did my mother, he did not deny the abuse.

I was relieved, because there had been a great deal of reporting in the papers and magazines during the 1980s of the 'memory wars.' This was a time when medical professionals, particularly in the United States, were reporting that survivors of childhood sexual abuse had repressed the memories of these events, but that they could be rekindled through psychoanalysis. What followed was a spate of false accusations and subsequent exonerations of those accused of abuse via this method. It began to throw into doubt the validity of claims of childhood sexual abuse.

I had moments when I imagined what a luxury it would be to have completely repressed the events of my past. Such blissful ignorance would have made my life easier.

But I had always known I had been abused. I was bereft of any periods of helpful amnesia.

Whilst he did not deny the abuse, my father was in denial about the significance of his behaviour, or how it could possibly have affected my life negatively. I remember him asking, 'Why didn't you tell me that you wanted it to stop?'

I wasn't able to articulate it then, but how on earth had I ever had a choice? I had never been given that option. I was only seven when the abuse began, for heaven's sake. If I had been able to opt out, this was the first I heard of it. What my father perpetrated on my innocent body had never seemed like a voluntary activity.

As a child, I worried about making him angry. He did not rise to anger easily or often, but when he did, it was terrible and terrifying.

So I became a people pleaser. I made sure everyone was happy—there was no discord, and no-one was upset. That was all part of keeping the family together. Harmony was everything. Harmony was unifying.

But my silence had not served me—or my family—well.

As the days and weeks unfolded, it became clear that keeping The Secret had only delayed the inevitable and awful exposing of the past.

In the weeks and months that followed, the revelations kept on coming. As though by way of an aside or afterthought (or perhaps an explanation?), my father told us that as a young child, he had been sexually abused by the family maid. Many years later, I researched this cycle of child sexual abuse and found studies that indicated many male perpetrators were themselves abused as children. It seems that abuse by a female during childhood appears to be a greater risk factor for creating a cycle of abuse in adult males who go on to perpetrate the same on younger people.

At times I have wondered whether my fate was preordained.

My brothers were told of my abuse (some years later), but not by me. I only found out their reactions much later. Apparently, they were in a state of disbelief that my father could have done such a thing. He had always been held on such a high pedestal, giving the impression that he was an exemplary father and husband.

They were broken. The true story of who we were as a family caused all previous images to be shattered.

Over that period when everything came out, I could not believe what was happening.

I had never wanted anyone in my family to know about The Secret and had worked hard to ensure no-one did. I did not reveal it to a single friend from high school or university, nor even my husband, until a couple of months earlier.

I had lived my life believing I had dealt with it on my own and that I would do so for the rest of my life. So much time had passed—if I could have kept The Secret during those childhood years, what was the point of revealing it now? It could serve no purpose other than to cause hurt and distress to the people I loved.

So I coped in the only way I knew how—I went back to silence.

I refused to talk about it.

I wanted everyone to move on and pretend it had never happened—both the abuse and its revelation. It was all too hard. The conversations were awkward and felt pointless. Nothing could be done to change the past, and how could it matter in the present?

What would happen if people outside the family found out? We had all established ourselves in our own communities. My father was still practising medicine in a small country town. My mother was involved in volunteer work and had earned respect and social standing. My brothers had their careers and were well regarded in their spheres of expertise.

Everyone's status in society seemed to matter—it had always mattered—and the revelation did not make a difference.

No-one ever spoke about taking punitive actions against my father. There was never any mention of the police or criminal charges.

It wasn't an option.

This was the family's business—a taboo that was kept in-house, in the family. And that's how everyone wanted it to stay.

I wondered how many others had lived with this same secret hidden in the walls of the family home and kept within the confines of their darkest places? How much damage had been caused by this deeply held secret, so long buried, interred beneath an insurmountable mound of shame, guilt and self-loathing? How many people were out there, wondering what was wrong with them? How many had found that their secrecy had manifested in fear, anger and even illness because of this taboo of which they could never—dare not—speak?

In the wake of this exposure, our lives should have been changed forever.

But over the next few years, members of my family fell into their usual routines, and everyone behaved much as they had always done. The outside world still had no idea of our sordid past and its recent upheaval. Business went on as usual, as did life and the lie of happy families.

The sun felt good on my skin as I lay on the sunlounge beside the large free-form hotel pool, reading a nondescript glossy magazine. It was the mid 1990s when we travelled to the Gold Coast regularly to spend the weekend at a five-star hotel. The area was largely deserted, and the quiet was only disturbed by the occasional screeching of a lone cockatoo.

Suddenly, the silence was filled with the sound of a terrified child screaming. I looked up to see a woman and a young child in the water. She was not only encouraging him to swim towards her unaided but was forcing him to swim against his will.

'No, no. I don't want to. I'm scared, Mummy,' he pleaded. 'I want to get out. I don't want to swim.'

'Come on. You have to learn to swim whether you're scared or not. It's important that you can swim so you don't drown. Don't be a baby—you're a big boy now,' she insisted.

As the child's screams became high pitched and frantic, I felt my stomach knotting and began to shake my head disapprovingly.

She continued to criticise and insist he keep trying to swim.

Powerless, I felt the bile climbing in my throat. By now, I was visibly distressed and continued to shake my head at this scene unfolding in front of me.

The woman then pulled her child out of the pool, left him with his father and began to swim across the pool heading straight towards my chair.

'Excuse me,' she said, looking up at me.

I continued to flick through the pages of my magazine, not wanting to engage with this aquatic tyrant.

'Yes, I'm talking to you,' she said harshly.

I peered at her from beneath my sunhat, making reluctant eye contact with her.

'Do you have children?'

I was so taken aback all I could do was stare at her. 'Well, do you?' she persisted.

I shook my head.

'Well, then you have no right to judge how I'm teaching my son to swim. I've been told by an expert that this is what is needed, that he has to get past these fears. And if that means he gets upset, I just have to keep going.'

Looking back, there is so much I should have said, but all I managed was, 'Well, it is very noisy and unsettling.'

'Oh, so this is all about your peace and quiet being disturbed, isn't it?' And with a snort and harumph, she swam off.

I could hardly breathe. Tears welled up in my eyes. I grabbed my stuff and hurried back to my room, where I began to sob. I was surprised by just how upset I was. Why had this strange woman and the bizarre treatment of her son had such an effect on me?

It was only much later that I realised what I should have said: 'I don't need to be a mother to be able to tell when a child is in distress and needs to be comforted rather than berated. I know that abusing children is unacceptable, and particularly if you are the person in the world most responsible for their safety and care.'

This woman thought I was judging her parenting in teaching her child how to swim—and maybe I was, but not in the way she imagined. What I saw was abuse.

From then on, I have become hyper-vigilant every time I witness interactions between parents and children, especially fathers playing with their young daughters.

I watch them sitting on laps, being cuddled and kissed and tickled, and I am immediately on alert. Feelings of dread weigh heavily in the pit of my stomach. I can't help wondering what all that public display of attention hides and whether that little girl has a secret life of abuse just as I did.

I also can't help myself from fearing that like me, she feels she has no-one to turn to or that she may not know that what happens to her in the night, when no-one is watching, is not normal. That it is never how fathers and daughters should behave.

So often I have been on the verge of speaking out but have stopped myself because I feel as if I have no right to interfere in other father-daughter relationships. I have no experience of what a loving, non-abusive interaction between a father and daughter is, devoid of anything sinister.

But no matter how many times I tell myself that, I still can never shake those feelings of concern. It's taken a long time, but I have finally come to accept that my childhood experiences affected my desire and willingness to bring a child into the world. My decision may have been especially influenced by the events of 1986. At a time of my life when I might have considered having a child, my secret had its first public airing. It was an emotionally charged time, with deep-seated feelings laid bare and open to scrutiny.

In that year, as well as the dozen years that followed, my life was full of shame, guilt, regret, reburying of emotions, game-playing of 'family business as usual' and the habitual physical manifestation of losing and regaining large amounts of weight. I wonder if I was so emotionally spent, and my resilience had been so completely drained that I had no capacity to even consider taking on a project that required making such a total commitment to another human being.

There have been times in my life when others have found my choice to remain child-free to be 'selfish.' But I have come to understand that it was a decision about self-preservation—a life jacket to enable my exhausted self to survive in a sea of self-doubt and uncertainty.

This means that I am often the only woman of my age in a room who does not have children and nowadays, grandchildren. Just for good measure, I have never been a fur-baby person either. A woman in her sixties without children and pets, puts me in a miniscule percentage of the population.

I imagine that the newspaper reports of my demise will read, 'A 100-year-old widow, having lived a long and healthy life, died peacefully at home. She was childless and the lack of kitty litter or tins of Chum suggested a lonely, unaccompanied old age.'

19
A WOMAN AMONG MEN

'You look good sitting in that seat, behind the wheel. Really suits you.' The salesperson was all charm and white teeth.

'It's nice to dream.'

'We can make this happen for you. I'm able to offer really favourable terms. Let me show you how that would work.'

'Just looking.' I slipped off the seat and headed back to the dock. This was madness. There was no way we could afford a brand-new boat loaded with extras. This was like the boats you see in the movies. We headed back to our island after our visit to the Airlie Beach Boat Show.

A week later, I received a call. 'I'm wondering if you're still interested in buying a boat.'

'It's way too expensive for us. Thanks for your call, but we'll need to leave it at that.'

'What if I knocked the price down and gave you the option of paying the boat off over six months?'

'What numbers are we talking about?'

He mentioned a figure which was a considerable reduction on the original asking price. We were now playing a game, and I had nothing to lose by making a counter-offer at an even lower price. This would surely put an end to the game playing.

'Woah! That's a lot lower than I'm authorised to accept. How about I speak to my boss and see what I can do?'

'Sure.' I didn't expect to hear from him again.

A day later, he called back.

'If you still want that boat, it's yours. My boss has accepted your offer.'

Suddenly, we had gone from tyre kickers (or the boat equivalent) to the potential owners of a very classy, brand-new 24' Mustang Sports Cruiser.

I gathered my thoughts and asked the question I thought would end the negotiations.

'And we still have six months to pay it off?'

I imagined those pursed lips and clenched perfect teeth, but clearly heard, 'Yes, that will be fine.'

So after a trip to Townsville to pay a deposit and tow the boat back to Shute Harbour, we were now the proud owners of this 'toy.'

I was the captain, and John was the crew. He did all the jobs that I didn't want to do like hosing the boat down after a cruise, refuelling and getting it out of the water and onto the trailer so it could be towed back to the storage yard.

All I had to do was drive—and I had always liked to be in the driver's seat.

'Come closer so you can hear me,' the loud hailer called out to ninety-eight escort boat captains on the

ACT 3 — A WOMAN AMONG MEN

Hamilton Island docks.

'The weather is fine for the rest of the day. The seas are moderately choppy, especially on the far side of Dent Island, where your teams will have their first changeover. I know this is a race, but safety comes first. With nearly a hundred teams, there will be almost three hundred people in the water at the same time, all within a few hundred metres of each other. You all have your written instructions. Make sure you and the crew have read them thoroughly. We have never had an accident in this race, and we want to keep it that way. If you have any questions, come and see me now.'

The dock was awash with boat captains and outrigger paddlers. This was the highlight of the four-day outrigger carnival—the forty-two kilometre marathon. Crews from Tahiti, Hawaii, New Zealand and every state of Australia had descended on the island for this annual event.

Due to the length of the race, crews were permitted to have changeovers at set points on the course. This meant that a crew of six would commence the race, and three alternate paddlers would be dropped into the sea, ready for the changeover. Three paddlers would literally fall overboard from the outrigger, and the three paddlers in the water would immediately haul themselves into the boat. The speed with which the more experienced crews did this manoeuvre was extraordinary—it all happened in just a few seconds.

Finding ninety-eight escort boats, and people to captain them, was an annual challenge for the organisers. Escort boats had to meet a list of criteria before they could be entered into the race, without which the paddlers were without a support crew for the event. If that were to happen, the original crew of six would have to complete the entire race, with no substitutions.

On this particular day, I had volunteered my services and my boat for the event.

I was assigned a crew—the Senior Masters Men's team from Hawaii. This was an honour. The oldest member of this crew had been paddling for over sixty years and was a legend among the younger paddlers.

Following the briefing, captains and paddlers were heading to their boats, readying for departure. I could see the three allocated crew members, whom I had met the previous night, making their way towards me through the crowd. Although senior in age, their fitness was comparable to that of much younger men, and their experience was evidenced in the lines on their faces and the callouses on their hands.

We shoved off from the dock. I had decided to take a friend, an experienced paddler well-known to the Hawaiians. The five of us headed out to sea, towards the first changeover point on the far side of Dent Island.

I felt confident in my ability to handle my craft in the sea conditions, but the challenge was to ensure that our three passengers were dropped off in exactly the right spot for the outrigger boat to find them and effect the necessary changes of crew. I had to execute this safely while remaining conscious that ninety-seven other boat captains were doing the same exchange within metres of one another. There were hundreds of paddlers in the water, hundreds more flipping out of their canoes, and every one of them needed to be picked up and moved on to the next changeover point.

I have no idea how I got through those four hours. There were times when the knots in my stomach tied themselves into larger knots, but I had voluntarily taken on this responsibility, and people's lives were in my hands. The sea around each of the changeovers was like a scene from a *Pirates of the Caribbean* movie, where the Kraken begins to churn the water and threaten the ship with annihilation. On more than one occasion, I found myself feeling ill. I was a seasick ship's captain. Ironic.

At all times, I needed to be in control, know exactly what the boat would do and where my crew members were in the water as well as everyone else's. I was out of my depth—literally. But I could not admit this to anyone. It was yet another instance when I took on a role and got through it by acting the part.

After hours in churning water, feeding and watering wet crew members as they came onto my boat to ready themselves for their next turn, ensuring every changeover was as smooth as possible and each water-bound man was safely extracted from the sea, I was exhausted. But the race was done.

As the final set of crew members took over the canoe and headed to the shore of Cat's Eye beach, I motored back to the marina to secure the boat. It had been a difficult but amazing experience.

It was then I had a dawning realisation.

I had done it to myself—again. I had entered a field dominated by men. Men were boat captains, not women. Men bought boats and negotiated tough prices, usually with other men. Men took other men out to sea. And now I was alone among a sea of men—literally.

Only one of the ninety-eight escort boats had a female captain.

Like my forays into cricket, karate, the Army Reserve, my love of sports cars and even the fact that I proposed to John (and the helicopter flying that was yet to come)—I seemed to pursue activities traditionally dominated by men.

I wondered on that day why I always felt as if I had to prove myself as being equal to or better than a man? Why was that so important?

Had my childhood experiences forced me to turn away from my femininity, to get in touch with my masculine side? Would being more manly make me less sexually appealing and therefore, less vulnerable?

Or were all my achievements simply attempts to make my father proud of me, show him that I was strong and capable and unafraid, in spite of all he had taken from me?

If that was so, did it mean that I perceived women as weak and men as strong?

I had never had these thoughts during my childhood or the years that followed. It was only later, as I reflected on the patterns of my life, that I wondered why I was so determined to be different from the other girls and women in my life.

From such an early age, I had felt I was unique—that there was nobody else like me. Convincing myself of this specialness, I had created a life of glorious martyrdom—a Saint Joan for the twentieth century. I might not have died for my cause, but it was true that a part of me—my childhood—had never really been given the chance to live.

AN EXPAT EXPERIENCE

On a hot and humid night, I arrived in the Seychelles. The heat, even at 3am was oppressive and stifling, and the smell from the world's largest tuna canning factory all pervasive. I had just accepted a job as the Human Resources Manager of an exclusive island resort, just three degrees below the equator, after two successful interviews via Skype. It was a huge adventure and a great leap of faith.

The disembarking humans were lined up, awaiting our turn at the immigration counter. We all participated in the slow-footed shuffle, where the forward movement of the human millipede, even if only by a few inches, is regarded as a major achievement—one small step for a man, one giant leap for the traveller.

It is also a well-known fact of travelling that the number of immigration counters open to process incoming passengers will be in inverse proportion to the actual number required. And the presence of a long line, populated by tetchy, agitated people, seems in no way to encourage the members of that country's officialdom to move any faster, nor seek the assistance of additional colleagues to hasten the process. It is as though there is a new time continuum, where all movements are seen through a slow-motion camera.

The taking of the passport from the hands of the traveller, the flicking of the pages to confirm the identity, a meaningful stare by the official at the incoming microbe standing in front of them, a searching glance over their counter to find the necessary date stamp (that was only moments ago in their hand for the self-same purpose), the deliberate measured pressing of that rubber imprint onto the chosen page, and the torturous closing and handing back of this most precious document. This procedure is universal, regardless of race or culture.

When humans are forced into this close proximity, where interpersonal space is challenged at every step, their behaviours become specific to the occasion. Some shore up their real estate with suitcases front and back, daring marauders to infiltrate their well-protected fortress. Others are distracted, accessing phone messages and emails on their electronic device, from which they have suffered withdrawal during the long flight. This causes the line ahead to move forward—without them. The annoyed sighs and meaningful glances from those behind finally attract the attention of the absent-minded one, and with guilty looks and much shoving of suitcases, they shuffle up to the end of the line.

The fact that they have only missed a movement of three feet and that everyone still has a long wait until they reach the head of the queue is immaterial. There is an unspoken code, an unwritten law—if you do your part in the line, as a member of the collective conscious, the universe is in order.

I finally arrived at the counter, hot and sweaty and very tired. As I handed my passport and letter of introduction from my employer to the equally hot, sweaty and tired official, I noticed that it was unsigned. I thought to myself, 'This might be a problem,' and so it was.

This first encounter with a Seychelles' person was fraught with confusion and bewilderment on his part. He peered at me, perused my passport and scanned both sides of the one-sided letter. He repeated this manoeuvre several times, but there were no changes to me, my passport or the letter. Finally, I was advised to 'stay there,' while he left his post and went in search of others. The groan from the queue behind me was loud and not unreasonable. It was clearly my fault that there was now one less immigration officer to assist with our entry into the country.

He returned and asked, 'So who are you meeting here?'

'A man called Thomas is meant to be here with his taxi to take me to my apartment. I am going to Tortoise Island in about four hours.'

'You are going to Tortoise Island?'

'Yes, to Tortoise. Like it says in the letter.'

He stared at the letter again. 'Come with me.' He headed off in the direction of the airport exit. I followed, trying to keep him in sight as we weaved our way through the thronging crowd. I worried about how and when I would get my luggage.

We were soon outside the airport on the footpath into the steamy morning. As the sweat dripped from my nose, we headed to the taxi rank, where a line of mismatched vehicles waited patiently. My official pointed at me and then pointed to the drivers leaning on their cars and mingling in small groups. 'Tortoise Island, Tortoise Island,' he called to no-one in particular.

This caused much chatter and enquiry among themselves and then a man came forward and said, 'Tortoise Island.' He was better dressed than the others, and I felt encouraged by his smile.

My minder asked, 'Is this one yours?'

And although we had never met, and he had no photo of me, this new man looked me up and down and still smiling, said, 'Yes, she's mine.'

Clearly, I was the only Caucasian female arriving at 3am that morning for a twelve-month stay on Tortoise Island. So with this man's acknowledgement of my existence and his verification of my credentials, I was taken back through the airport to the original immigration desk, where my passport was stamped, and I was officially allowed to enter the country.

Despite being forty-seven years old and settled in a twenty-year marriage, I was still seeking new professional experiences. I had come to the Seychelles to fulfil a new goal—to live the life of an expat. I had never worked overseas in my chosen profession and had a completely romanticised view of what that life would be like.

In the coming weeks, my idealised picture of this position would come to bear no resemblance to reality. There would be no community of like-minded, culturally compatible colleagues who met on a regular basis for cocktails.

Instead, I would find that I was the only white female staff member on the island; there was a chaotic change of leadership underway; most of the staff were miserable; resignations were at an all-time high; and the only other staff member in the human resources team was about to be offered the job of assistant front office manager.

My predecessor had said he was unable to stay any longer than the very last day of his agreed contract. He would not be able to provide me with any kind of handover.

It was clear he could not get out of there fast enough. I was soon to learn the reasons for his rapid departure.

~

'He said that if I slept with him, I would get all sorts of privileges. I would get better food than the other staff, and my shifts would be changed so that I got an extra day off each week. I have been sleeping with him for weeks, and none of those things have happened.'

The tall, elegant young woman standing in my office was an African beauty. She was one of the Kenyan staff who had come to Tortoise Island on a two-year contract. Her demeanour and bearing belied her eighteen years.

She took a deep breath and stared into my eyes. In spite of this startling news, she was remarkably calm and measured. It was as though we were speaking of a simple business transaction—she had entered into the arrangement in good faith, and he had not kept his part of the bargain.

'I am worried that if I stop having sex with him, he will get angry and say bad things about me on the island. He might even arrange to have me sent back to Kenya.'

Whilst I wanted to reassure her that her employment could not be terminated by this man or for these reasons, I wondered if that was a very real possibility. *We ain't in Kansas anymore, Toto.*

I asked her what she wanted me to do.

'I want him to know that he cannot treat people this way. He told me that I was special and that he would take care of me, but he has lied. He needs to know that this is wrong. I want to stop sleeping with him, but I want to keep my job.'

Although I had been on the island for only a few days, others had already made me aware of the relationship between this young woman and one of the senior managers, a white South African man who had lived and worked on Tortoise for many years. I was advised that she was not the first young woman who had found herself in the circumstances she was now describing to me.

I knew I would have to confront this man with the allegations of sexual misconduct and intimidation which she had made. He and I had spoken only twice and each time, in the presence of other island managers. From those meetings, I learned that his extended time on the island had given him a level of implied seniority which far exceeded his job description. He was regarded by the other male managers as the *bwana*, the top of the management food chain. This sense of entitlement was evidenced by the way he strutted around the island, as though daring others to challenge him for the role of alpha male.

When I advised the general manager that I wanted to have a conversation with this man about an important staff complaint, he said, 'Well, good luck with that,' and walked away, not the least interested in the nature of the issue. I was on my own.

As I waited in the boardroom for him to arrive, I fiddled with my pen and notebook on the table, as if rearranging them again and again would make this meeting go more smoothly.

He barged through the door like a bull, as if announcing his role as head of the island's ecology department across his tanned, sweating face. He towered over me.

'I am not used to being summonsed to appear before people, and certainly not by a woman. This had better be something important.' His words left his lips like bullets from a machine gun.

I gestured to a chair, and he threw himself into it, causing it to teeter on its back two legs. This caused him to be temporarily unsettled, but he quickly regrouped and pulled the chair up to the table with a meaningful thud.

I got straight to the point. 'A most serious allegation regarding your behaviour has been brought to my attention, and as HR manager, I am required to have a conversation with you about it.'

He looked up to the ceiling, his eyes rolling back in his head, and surprisingly, began to laugh.

'Oh, God. What am I supposed to have done now?' I sensed this was not the first time his misconduct had been brought to his attention.

'Well, a young woman has come to see me, alleging that you promised her all sorts of benefits if she, um, slept with you.'

I was certainly not prepared for his response.

'That's right. Each year, I take one of the new girls as my partner. She comes and lives in my accommodation, has sex with me and I make sure that her life is a little easier. I am actually doing her a big favour.'

It was all I could do to stop my eyes from popping out of my head. Calmly, this man was confirming the 'business transaction' of my earlier conversation.

'So you are admitting that you are offering improved housing and working conditions for sex?'

'My dear girl, you have no idea how things work around here. You have been here five minutes. I have lived my whole life in Africa—Zimbabwe, Kenya, South Africa—and the Seychelles. TIA, TIA, TIA.'

It would be another twelve months before I saw Leonardo DiCaprio's *Blood Diamond*, where that acronym became a critical part of the story. But for now, this was a new experience for me.

He noticed my blank looks and said slowly, as though speaking to a child, 'This is Africa. This is Africa. If you are not African, you cannot understand. And you certainly have no authority to speak on African matters.'

He stood up. From his point of view, we were done. I was not about to let him leave the room. I knew this meeting would be the benchmark for my credibility and authority in the coming months. I needed to take charge of the moment.

'This conversation is not over. Please sit down.'

I pointed at the chair and stared straight into his eyes.

He seemed surprised, but he shrugged and sat.

'The staff member is claiming that you sexually harassed her until she agreed to sleep with you. She only did it because of the favours you promised, and now she says that you have reneged on that promise.'

'She is eighteen years old—a woman. She is able to make up her own mind about who she sleeps with. I am not making her do anything she didn't want to do.'

'So you don't think the fact that you are a senior manager on this island, whose authority and influence far exceeds her own, should be taken into account when considering relationships with more junior staff?'

'Like I said, she is a grown woman and can make her own choices.'

'I disagree. The power imbalance between your roles means that she is fearful of displeasing you and incurring negative consequences. She believes that keeping her role on the island is dependent on keeping you happy. That should not be the case.'

For the first time, he began to look uncomfortable, but was no less determined.

'Look, I will not be lectured by you on who I can and cannot sleep with. This is an arrangement between two consenting adults, and quite frankly, it is none of your goddamn business.'

I took a deep breath and contemplated my next words. Of course, on one level, he was right. I had no right to dictate the sex life of the adults on the island. I was taking a very hard line on this issue, and I asked myself why this mattered so much to me. What had this triggered for me?

I was rapidly losing control of the situation but was determined not to back down.

'Well, she has lodged a formal complaint with me, and I am advising you that this is a form of sexual harassment that is unacceptable in the workplace. I am asking that you think about the effects that you've had on this young woman and her time on the island. You need to consider this from her point of view.'

My tenacity paid off. He realised I was not going to let the matter drop and that he was going to have to rethink his attitude towards younger female staff members.

'All right, all right. I have heard what you've had to say. I will be more careful in the future.'

As I was congratulating myself on this major breakthrough, he continued, 'More careful to choose a girl who understands the rules of our arrangement and doesn't come blabbing to management just because the relationship comes to an end.'

With that, he stood up, gave a wry smile and left the room.

I was exhausted. It had been such a gruelling session and so early in my time on the island.

Once again, I was left feeling powerless and without any control over a situation of abuse.

Power—it was all about power. He had so much; she had so little. It didn't seem fair that she had found herself in this position, and I desperately wanted to save her.

If only someone had been able to save me all those years ago. But there had been no-one to talk to, no-one in my corner.

And unlike this brave young woman who had brought her concerns to me, knowing there could be serious consequences, I had been too afraid to stand up for myself, too afraid of the imagined consequences.

I left the room fighting back tears—not only for the beautiful young African woman but also for that little girl, who, even now, still needed to be saved.

COMING HOME

Within three weeks, I was lonely, homesick and ready to leave the island. But I'd signed a twelve-month contract, so it was impossible. I had a track record of resilience and fortitude that would allow me to cope with these new and difficult circumstances. *Suck it up, sunshine. You were the one who wanted this overseas experience.*

I spent the evenings alone in my room, crying and wishing I was back in Australia. The other managers on the island were all males who spent their time together drinking copious quantities of alcohol and talking about fishing, a popular pastime on the island.

Not only was I socially isolated, I found the European managers of the island had very little understanding of the culture of the Seychellois and the management style required to encourage commitment to their roles. This was essential as guests had the highest expectations of excellent service from our team—not unreasonable given they were paying the extraordinary sum of three thousand five hundred euros per night.

I was struggling to sleep, my uniform was getting very tight and I didn't want to speak to John on the Skype calls we arranged.

It would have been unprofessional to resign only weeks into the job, so I needed to find a legitimate reason to leave the island.

Then I came up with an idea which in retrospect reveals my desperation. At the time, it seemed like a stroke of pure genius.

I decided to *find* a lump in my breast. I knew no one would question such a personal discovery. I would use the suggestion of breast cancer as my legitimate exit strategy from the island.

The following day, I mentioned this to one of the senior female supervisors on the island. I imagined returning to the civilisation of the Western world to seek all manner of medical expertise for my problem. Thinking clearly was not my strong suit at this time.

She informed me that the doctor on Mahe had an ultrasound machine and was quite capable of ascertaining whether or not I had a lump in my breast.

This was not part of my plan. I wanted to go home. This was meant to be my ticket home.

But after only a few moments of rational thought, it was clear. Of course, he would have such facilities—there were lots of women in the Seychelles. They couldn't all head out of the country to have their breasts examined.

So the following week, in order to carry out this subterfuge and take it to the next level, I travelled on the helicopter's empty leg to the capital and borrowed a car from the Tortoise Island staff based there. I drove out to the doctor's clinic and sat in the overcrowded, noisy waiting room. The children were running amok but would stop and stare as they passed me. They pointed at my face and giggled, while their mothers shushed them and pulled them back to their seats. My white face stood out in the sea of brown—it was my first experience of being a minority race.

The doctor was an older man with world-wearied lines that etched his coffee-brown face. In spite of the chaos in the waiting room, he was calm and welcoming.

He took me into a side room and handed me a short gown.

'Please remove your blouse and bra and put this on. It does up at the front. Once you have done that, lie down on this bed and I'll be back in a moment.'

He left the room and seemed to be gone for some time. Eventually, he returned, wheeling in the ultrasound machine.

He was methodical in his examination. I had created this lump as a distraction and as a method of escaping from my own version of Alcatraz, but it occurred to me that anything was possible. As this was my first ever breast examination, there might actually be something there. That would be ironic.

But he found nothing.

'You have very fibrous breasts, and so they will often feel quite lumpy. I think that is all you felt— there is nothing sinister here.'

Of course, I was relieved that I didn't have anything wrong with my breasts; but my desperate, homesick self so hoped that there might be a legitimate reason to leave the Seychelles and go home.

As I flew back to the island, I decided that I needed to regroup. 'You are not a quitter. You need to see this through. What is wrong with you? Trying to create an awful medical condition just because you are way out of your comfort zone and now you are resorting to extreme solutions. You are better than this. You have always been better than this.'

By the time I landed, I had devised a much better plan. I would work hard for the next three months. After that, if I still felt that I wanted to go home, I would give the management of the resort three months' notice. During that time, I would recruit and appoint my replacement. I would ensure she or he was inducted into the role and into the ways of the island— an opportunity I was not given by my predecessor. Once that was all in place, I could legitimately head back to Australia, my professionalism and honour intact.

I wandered back from the helipad to my apartment. Now in the company of cool and rational decision-making, it seemed so ludicrous that I had actually been trying to wish that I had breast cancer. What sort of woman does such a thing to herself?

Years later, I would have cause to remember that lonely time in a country far away. A time when I had disrespected that dreadful disease. Was it possible to incur the wrath of powers greater than ourselves?

It was truly a case of, *'Be careful—so very careful— what you wish for.'*

THE DIAGNOSIS

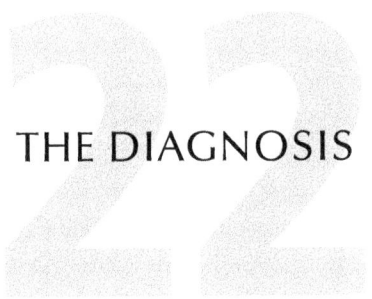

'This one is not nearly as interesting as that one.'

The sonographer from BreastScreen Queensland had just finished scanning my left breast and was now pointing towards its twin.

That did not sound good. I was having a series of new scans and tests after a phone call the previous week, asking me to come back after my routine mammogram.

I was due to finish working for the University of the Sunshine Coast when I got the call. In three weeks, at the age of fifty-six, I would be starting a new role at another university, in another state.

'The doctors have seen something on your scans that is, um, unusual, and they would like you to come in and have it checked out,' said the nurse who had called me. Her voice was hushed, giving away her discomfort.

I had squeezed the phone tightly, fearing it would drop. After four successive negative breast screening visits, now there was a problem. I had no time in my life for any problems, and certainly not the one that could be implied by this news. Over the coming days, as I waited for my appointment, I wondered, *What if? Surely not?* There was no history of breast cancer in our family. I told myself to remain calm. No diagnosis had been made—I simply had to go back for more tests.

Naughty knocker, shitty titty, burst bust, ruined rack, unfit tit—boob flu. From the time of that phone call, I began to create these *nom de plumes*, writing them on scraps of paper, saying them out loud. This flippancy was how I made the reality of the situation less real, easier to manage, a trait I had perfected over my lifetime.

At the clinic, I had a second mammogram on a machine that was capable of providing a higher degree of magnification than the one used for my regular scans. This time, my breast was pressed and flattened further. It lay there on the glass plate looking like one of those blobfish that live on the ocean floor.

That was followed by an ultrasound. The sonographer covered the probe in gel and took a great deal of time and care in covering every square centimetre of my boobs. And now one of them was 'interesting.'

But I did not want interesting breasts. I wanted completely bland ones, just as they had always been. These were D-grade students, actually double D to be precise. They had arrived at the end of primary school and were the debutantes of my class, a novelty to everyone—school chums male and female, and especially to me. I went shopping for bras while others played with Barbies. These frontal appendages and I were well acquainted. We knew one another's foibles and preferences—we had hung out together for a long time.

I wondered what she was seeing. What did a lump look like?

Later, I saw the ultrasound. I literally saw nothing but a black hole, with blacker tentacles reaching out into the breast tissue—a Crown of Thorns starfish, eating breasts instead of coral. I was being invaded—from the inside. Like the alien that rose up through the earth in the *War of the Worlds*—it had been hidden, waiting to strike, and now its time had come.

What do you do after five hours at the breast clinic, toting around a punctured boob—a biopsy had been necessary—and probably a dose of breast cancer? You go to lunch, naturally.

John and I pulled into the car park of a favourite restaurant, discussing the menu and our possible lunch choices. It occurred to me that the ice pack had now been in place for the requisite thirty minutes and could be removed. As I lifted the package out of my bra and into the daylight, I was suddenly aware that the white cover was now red. Then I became conscious of blood dripping down my side, through my shirt and down my arm. I was bleeding profusely from the biopsy site.

It was now clear that lunch was not going to happen. I rang the clinic in Nambour—the phone went to message bank. I rang my GP—that phone also went to message bank (it was their golfing half day, of course). With tears welling in my eyes and my options running out fast, I instructed John to drive to the emergency department (ED) of the Caloundra Hospital. As I was clearly bleeding to death, they would have all the necessary equipment to administer a blood transfusion, which evidently, I would be requiring.

We arrived at the front door of the ED, and I strode purposely to the front counter, producing bloodied icepacks and a blood-soaked shirt, which moved me straight to the front of the line.

'You had better come through,' said the duty nurse, displaying a high level of calm and nonchalance.

I had better come through, all right, I thought to myself. *I am exsanguinating. If I don't get immediate attention, I am going to bleed to death right here.*

Once in the examination room, I lifted my bloodied shirt and removed my bra to reveal the bloodied bandaged biopsy site from which blood was dripping down.

Her next words were indicative of the chasm between medical staff and non-medical patients.

'Ah,' she said. 'You do have a bit of ooze.'

'Ooze?' I said. 'Ooze! Surely, it is more serious than that?'

'Well,' she said, 'that is all that has happened here. There has been some bleeding from the biopsy site. Were you holding that icepack firmly against the wound?'

I had to think about this. Actually, if I had to describe how I had been holding the icepack, firmly was not a word I would have used. However, in my defence, I did not remember being asked to hold it firmly.

'Well, kind of firmly, I suppose,' I answered weakly.

'Hmm,' she said. 'Well, just take this padding and hold it against the biopsy site *firmly* for the next thirty minutes. It will stop bleeding, and you will be fine.'

By now, she had lost interest in me and my blood. I was clearly an interloper, an ED cheat who had gotten into her inner sanctum through foul means.

I redressed with my bloodied bra and bloodier shirt, pressed the bandage as instructed, and left, like a child with a graze, who just needed a Band-Aid to make it all better.

This was the first in a series of medical procedures in the coming days and weeks.

Two days later, we were back at Nambour hospital, where the results of that bloody biopsy confirmed what I already knew. This time, The Darkness was not an external visitor but came from deep inside.

I wondered if this silent invader had, in fact, been present for many years—sitting below the surface, hidden by the complexity and density of my breast tissues. It had festered covertly for many years and now had chosen to reveal itself. Was it the physical manifestation of a secret held too deeply for far too long?

In the months and years that followed during my treatment for breast cancer, I began to make the connections between my physical illness and my psychological wound.

Like a lump in a breast, the cancer of my childhood abuse also needed to be identified, acknowledged, diagnosed, removed and treated. But the treatment to heal that would be ongoing.

I have learned that some secrets should be uncovered as soon as possible so that their timely discovery can lead to earlier intervention. Tissues can be navigated and exposed by a surgeon's scalpel and blasted with chemicals. If only other traumas could be handled so efficiently.

The old axiom states that there are two certainties in life—death and taxes. And if you have a good accountant, or happen to be Donald Trump, you can get away with not paying the latter. So in fact, the only certainty in life is death. The diagnosis of breast cancer made me pause and think about my life. And perhaps for the first time, my death.

I have never been 'good' with death. I am so afraid of this subject that I have spent many nights lying awake, pondering the life that may or may not exist after death. And because this is the unanswerable question, I find this both unproductive and distressing.

I had been so sheltered from death. I had never seen a dead body. In 2015, my mother and father were both still alive as well as my brothers, my sister, their spouses and children, all three of my mother's sisters, and their husbands, all my cousins and their spouses and children.

On the other hand, my husband had lost his father, mother, brother, brother-in-law, nephew, nephew-in-law and countless aunts and uncles. Some of these deaths had been traumatic, including suicides and brain tumours.

I attended these family funerals and was so distraught and inconsolable that I had needed to be comforted by the very people I was there to comfort. John's family have adopted a sanguine approach to the passing of loved ones. I always wanted to be like that—to be a person who gets that death is a part of life and who is able to attend a funeral without having to be held up by two people as I leave the church.

I suppose this is why we have created the concept of God and heaven and an afterlife—because we cannot conceive of the Great Nothing. And I so want there to be a heaven. I love the idea of sitting on a cloud, with a gathering of souls from the recent and ancient past, looking down on earth and chatting about the weather, or what those humans are doing down there and what we might have for lunch. But with no bodies, we won't need food. And if we are only souls, how would we communicate—telepathically? All this thinking becomes overwhelming, and I revert to being completely freaked out.

I have always been amazed at the elderly and terminally ill who say, 'I'm ready to go now.' I cannot imagine being in that place. I will *never* be ready to go, *ever*. I will still be okay even if I am in the process of dying because at least, I will not be dead. The very act of dying still suggests that you are alive and that is fine with me. Often, people have a DNR order in place when they are terminally ill—Do Not Resuscitate. My instructions are clear—RRR—Resuscitate Resuscitate Resuscitate.

But after my own brush with a life-changing and possibly fatal disease?

My views are unchanged.

23 THE TREATMENTS

When a friend was dealing with breast cancer, she refused to call her medical specialist 'my oncologist.' It was as if taking ownership of their title was an acceptance of her fate, the disease, and the fact that she had moved into a realm that was so dreadful, it required a high level of individualised medical specialisation and expertise. She decided to call him 'the doctor person.'

I, however, needed as many people as possible in my corner, and labelling a medical guru as mine gave me a level of comfort.

I was meeting *my* oncologist for the first time. I had been in Canberra only three weeks in which I'd made appointments with all the necessary members of the medical profession responsible for my treatment over a six-month period. In my spare time, I was undertaking the role of general manager at one of the academic colleges at the ANU, meeting and leading the eight managers who were my direct reports and getting to know the seventy staff who constituted my larger team. They knew nothing of the fact that I had arrived in a new city and into my new role ever so slightly *broken*, having *caught* a dose of breast cancer only seventeen days earlier.

I had created a picture of my oncologist before we met. As he had a double-barrelled surname and the title of Professor, all my instincts told me that he was unlikely to be an easy-going chap with a ready smile and a capacity for unfettered empathy. I should always go with my instincts.

Moments before I was due to meet the Prof, I had met my McGrath Breast Care Nurse, Kerryn. We had spent only a few moments together, but with her huge smile, engaging manner and obviously a sincere passion for the role she was undertaking, I already thought she was wonderful. I was very pleased that she was going to be with me for this appointment.

We sat side by side silently in his empty, clinical office. There was nothing to do but wait. After some time, his footsteps could be heard, and he strode through the door. Silver haired, slightly hunched and exuding an air of being short on time and clear of purpose.

As he walked towards his chair, and with barely a glance in my direction, he said, 'I think that you should have chemotherapy and, er, you will lose your hair.'

He had not even sat down. Nor had he introduced himself before he made this pronouncement. I wanted to stand up, put out my hand and say, 'Hello, my name's Louise. What's yours?' But I was too stunned. This was meant to be an initial meeting where we discussed my diagnosis and possible treatments. My surgeon had thought that radiation would be sufficient for my circumstances, without the need for chemotherapy. Clearly, having reviewed my file, as well as the size of my tumour and its rate of growth, the professor had decided I should undergo both types of treatment. But this course of action had not been in my early reckonings.

Faced with this new reality, the tensions of the past few weeks welled up inside, and I began to cry. I grabbed a tissue from the box on his desk. Immediately, I was disappointed in myself.

I had not cried once during the previous five weeks of enormous physical and psychological pressures. Not when they took the biopsy without waiting for the local anaesthetic to take effect so that it felt as though my breast was being passed through the eye of a needle. Not when I was told that the lump in my breast was cancerous—I had reconciled myself to that fate two days earlier, when the biopsy was taken. Not when I left my husband at the airport and travelled to Canberra alone to begin this new work challenge—I wanted the new job so much, and it had never occurred to me to ring the ANU and tell them that I had breast cancer and would be unable to take up the role. I was determined to start on the day I had agreed in my contract, signed several weeks before the cancer diagnosis.

I was so proud of this stoicism, of my resilience, of my capacity to do all that needed to be done without giving in to unhelpful emotions. I had become totally task focussed because that was how I rolled. This was how I had always dealt with the most stressful and traumatic moments of my life.

ACT 3 — THE TREATMENTS

But with this officious professor's words, I felt my world, the world where I was in charge and knew precisely what was happening, crumble around me. I was crashing to the floor, and like Humpty Dumpty, I was not sure that I would ever be put back together.

My life would never be the same again. It would always fall into two categories. There would be my own version of the years BC and AD—Before Cancer and After Diagnosis.

By contrast, the radiation oncologist was a delightful woman, who exuded warmth and kindness from every fibre of her vertically and horizontally challenged being. Her manner suggested that she really cared about her patients and their individual situations.

'Now I have read the report from the oncologist, the professor, and he has indicated that you will be having both chemotherapy and radiotherapy. He will be responsible for the former, and I will be responsible for the latter. So how much do you know about radiation, radiotherapy and its use in treating breast cancer?'

I had known that I had breast cancer for just over a month. During that time, I had been diagnosed, undergone a lumpectomy, been operated on again a week later to remove a massive infection, packed up my belongings into seven plastic boxes, arranged for those boxes and my car to be collected and transported to the ACT, flown to Canberra, installed myself in temporary accommodation and commenced my new job as a general manager at the Australian National University. I had already attended many meetings and encountered many staff, met a wonderful GP recommended by my surgeon, been allocated a breast care nurse, been shattered by the above-mentioned medical oncologist, travelled to Sale in Victoria to attend my nephew's graduation from the Air Force training school (stopping on the way to the airport at a local radiology clinic to have them drain a seroma, a pocket of fluid which had built up around the surgery site) and was now meeting Dr Lisa Sullivan. There had not been much time to conduct any research on my medical condition. It was fair to say that what I knew about this aspect of my treatment could have been printed on the back of what is rapidly becoming an obsolete cliché—a postage stamp.

'Not much,' I said.

She began to explain the role of this type of therapy and to outline the next stages in the process. Firstly, my breast would need to undergo a planning session. This would involve lying under a radiation simulator while my breast was mapped by the technicians. Cook, Vasco da Gama, Magellan—I was about to join this elite group of cartographers.

I would then be tattooed in three spots on the outer edges of my breast, enabling greater accuracy of the positioning of the machine which would be administering the doses of radiation—a linear accelerator. For those in the know, this is called a LINAC. Once my treatments began, I would sit in the waiting room with a dozen other patients, each of us allocated our ten-minute appointment time, having been designated a number from one to four, signifying our specific LINAC machine. We began to use this jargon like it was a part of our everyday vocabulary.

'Here,' said Lisa, showing me the inside of her wrist. 'Here is a tattoo, just like the ones you will have on your breast. As you can see, it is about the size of a freckle, and is really quite subtle.'

My first reaction to her revelation was not about the size, colour or shape of the tattoo. It was certainly an inoffensive mark that would be hardly noticeable, wherever it might be positioned on my breast. It was my instant admiration for this woman who was so committed to her craft and patients that she had permanently tattooed herself, just as her patients would be forever inked. It made me feel that we were in this together, and this sensitive and compassionate gesture was her way of saying, 'I know what you are going through, and I am right there with you.'

On planning day, a chirpy young woman led me into a room with a LINAC simulator. Imagining she was one of my therapists, I was surprised to discover that I was to be left in the room with three equally cheerful young male therapists. My expectations were dashed. Surely, breasts were a female matter; and therefore, all concerned with our hands-on treatment should be females. I was soon to learn that, in fact, the radiation specialists at the hospital were 50/50 men and women. My assumptions about the world of breast cancer were simply not true.

However, they could not have been more caring and considerate. They must have seen many thousands of women with breasts of all shapes and sizes, and probably had come to regard breasts simply as blobs that needed to be mapped and tattooed. Just as a baker would knead and mould bread dough into shape, these staff would move, lift and position breasts to ensure maximum coverage from the units of absorbed radiation that would be delivered by the LINAC.

When it came time for the tattooing, one of these young men did the job, advising me that it would feel like a pin prick and that he would be injecting a small amount of dye in the breast tissue.

'So having tattoos should give me a whole lot of street cred, huh?' I joked, but the lad just looked at me quizzically. Clearly, my sense of humour went way over his head.

The therapists then whispered among themselves. 'Are we ready? Shall we call her?' I wondered what was about to happen. One of them headed to a phone, announced into the mouthpiece that they were ready, and we waited together in complete silence. The sense of anticipation in the room hung over us all like children waiting for the fireworks countdown to begin on New Year's Eve.

Suddenly, Lisa appeared, and the acolytes moved away from me and huddled, reverentially, in a corner. This behaviour belied the jovial manner with which Lisa greeted me, but it was clear that the medical hierarchy was now in play; and in this department, the radiation oncologist was at the top of the pyramid.

It was now her turn to play with my boob. Her weapon of choice was a black felt-tip pen which she used to outline the field of play for the radiation therapists who would be performing my treatments in the coming weeks. She was friendly and professional but was gone in a moment—clearly, she had done this before. Next, the young men produced a large piece of tracing paper, which they placed over Lisa's artwork. They traced, with the utmost care and precision, with a finer felt-tipped pen. It was as though these students were copying the anatomical works of the master, and Lisa was their Leonardo da Vinci.

The final job was to create a 'cradle' for my back. This would ensure that I would be lying in exactly the correct position for each treatment and that my breast would be exposed to the radiation in the same way each time. This device was like a bean bag, filled with pellets, which was manipulated into the required shape. It was then marked with my name and details, and would be used at all thirty of my treatments.

I wondered where these devices were stored, given that there were hundreds of patients to be treated each day at the centre. Even if only half of us required such specialised adjustment, that was a lot of bulky, odd-shaped pieces of equipment that needed to be stored in close proximity to the LINAC rooms. And then what happened to them once my treatment was over, at the end of the six weeks? Were they thrown out? Could they be reconfigured for another patient?

I speculated that there was a cavernous room below the hospital in which superfluous 'cradles' were stored on racks that reached to the ceiling—rather like the scene in *Raiders of the Lost Ark*, when the box containing the Ark of the Covenant is placed into a massive storage room with hundreds of similarly marked boxes. In a thousand years, would archaeologists come across this find and wonder what significance they held for our now ancient society?

By the end of the appointment, I had been poked and prodded, tattooed, 'texta-ed' and had my own personalised back rest—and all this was just to get me ready for the treatments yet to begin. I felt as though my boobs were no longer my own but the property of the medical profession. It was the start of a new carefree relationship with my breasts and a laissez-faire attitude to their availability for future display—'Roll up, roll up. Come one, come all. See the bare-breasted, tattooed lady' (cue classic circus music).

THE AFTERMATH

My right boob was disintegrating. And not in a good way. Pieces of skin were falling from the underside of my breast. The previous week, there had been blisters in the gigantic fold where that mammary met my chest. Now those blisters had burst, and the skin was falling off in pieces. The area was red raw, and I did not have even a moment of painless peace.

'Ah.' The radiation nurse peered at the site now suffering from 'post-radiation stress disorder.' 'Well, that is actually quite common and to be expected, given the size and shape of your breasts. You know, it is not nearly as bad as I've seen on other people.'

At that very moment, I did not care one iota about other people. I cared about the fact that my under boob was extremely painful, was falling off in pieces and there seemed to be no solace. I did not want to have my suffering compared to others. In time, maybe I would be able to look back on this moment and make light of my circumstances, create jokes about my overhanging pendulous appendages and the consequences of their bulk. But at that moment, I wanted her to recognise that this was the worst thing that had ever happened to *my* boob, that this was *my* greatest pain ever and that these comparisons were absolutely not helpful.

The look on my face must have given her a clue. Soon, she was all care and concern, and other breast comparisons faded from the conversation.

'Here is some cream. It is the kind that we give mothers for babies with nappy rash. Just use lots of it. And here are some pads that you can wear so that your bra will not cause you any more grief than you are already experiencing.'

'Anything else that might help?'

'Try taking Panadol for the pain. Sometimes that works. See you tomorrow.'

After twenty-five successful radiation treatments, and with only five remaining, the consequence I had dreaded had eventuated and was very real. Once again, I was angry with my body. All the hard work had been done—the 'whole of the breast' radiation was complete. The five treatments yet to be undertaken would be directed only at the point of the lumpectomy, the spot from which the offending lump had been removed and would be nowhere near the underside of the nuked knocker.

I headed to the changing cubicle, cupping my right breast in order to reduce the effects of the inevitable bounce. I removed my gown and liberally applied the nappy rash cream to the space beneath the stinging fold. I placed the pad in the crevice, and I carefully manoeuvred my bra into position. As I finished dressing, I knew that no one was aware of the shedding that was taking place with every passing moment.

All was serene to the outsider, which was the way I wanted it. This dose of the boob flu was not going to define me.

MORE QUESTIONS THAN ANSWERS

Research findings suggest that cancer risk may be influenced by exposure to stressful conditions and events early on in life.

Childhood abuse is a risk factor for emotional problems after surgical treatment for breast cancer. The post-traumatic stress of this surgery may cause patients to recall the post-traumatic stress of earlier child abuse.

So there it was. I was a scientific and medical statistic.

As I began to recover from my breast cancer treatment, I began to ask myself some difficult questions. Had the years of childhood abuse contributed to my contracting breast cancer? Were those earlier stressors emerging from their dormancy, taking the form of this virulent disease? Was my breast cancer an inevitability over which I had no control? Had it been pre-ordained for the past fifty years?

At the time of my diagnosis and during the six months of my treatment, I was not aware of this correlation. I had done very little research into my condition. I was literally too busy for breast cancer, and I had simply done all that was required to treat the symptoms as they were presented.

But once I was made aware of this research, I had to ask myself—how did this make me feel? Was I even angrier with my father? Not only had I spent my childhood years being sexually abused by him, but there was a possibility that this abuse had given me breast cancer. It was a double blow—another betrayal.

At the time my breast cancer was diagnosed, I believed it was the consequence of my lifestyle choices over several years. I was, as usual, overweight. I exercised but not consistently and had climbed the corporate hierarchy, taking on more and more stressful roles. I was an ideal repository for an alien invasion and therefore, believed it was my fault that I had 'caught' breast cancer.

I had so often blamed myself for the abuse by my father, especially my lack of action to stop him and my determination to maintain The Secret at all costs. So it was easy to blame myself for the disease.

I wondered if it meant that all *bad* things that ever happened to me were my fault? Self-inflicted? Deserved?

It has taken me a long time, but I have come to understand that my breast cancer was a message from within. It forced me to look at what I had been holding on to and what I had buried beneath a superficial exterior. Mine was a lump that only a mammogram could find. No breast self-examination would have revealed its presence. Even the doctor, with both a mammogram and ultrasound as her guide, had difficulty finding it.

A machine—an inhuman, calculating, impersonal, objective machine—was needed to show me, bring it to my notice and force me to give it the attention it demanded.

This was a wake-up call of enormous proportions.

A SIZEABLE PROBLEM

'Started my diet today.' Four words in a diary entry. Five months later, *'Back on my diet.'*

It was 1972. I was thirteen-years-old.

Over the course of my life, it feels as though I have tried every weight loss programme, including, but certainly not limited to, Weight Watchers (several times, even becoming a lecturer in 1989), Jenny Craig (regularly since 1995), Lite n Easy (more often for the Easy than the Lite) and even Gloria Marshall. This company was all the rage in the 1980s. Its clients attended sessions at their premises several times a week. We had to use machines reminiscent of ancient implements of torture. One apparatus required you to kneel on the floor, while alternatingly pressing your belly or hips up against rotating wooden rollers. This was intended to displace and eradicate the fat. Another contraption was designed like the rack of medieval times. You held on tight, with your arms above your head, while the bed jumped and gyrated, like a horizontal bucking bronco. Lying there, watching your body fat move from side to side, was like watching an oversized plate of jelly being carried out to the dining table.

Of course, you were required to follow a low-calorie diet plan at the same time, and this was how the weight loss was truly achieved. Even knowing that, all of us women (I do not remember ever seeing a man in the salon) would turn up like well-trained hamsters to feed at the trough of hope.

Then there was the VLCD—Very Low-Calorie Diet— recommended by an eminent doctor from the United States. These diets were originally designed for the morbidly obese when all other weight loss methods failed. Often, dieters were hospitalised for the duration of the program. I ate only prescribed small amounts of food, weighed to the milligram. My average daily intake was only five hundred calories, less than half of that recommended for a healthy female adult. Of course, I lost eighteen kilos in fourteen weeks—I was actually following a starvation plan.

I have a great capacity for losing weight. I found that it would be most effective if I had a specific event that encouraged my resolve. A family wedding, a significant birthday, even a reunion. John and his Vietnam veteran buddies get together every three years, and I use that recurring anniversary to work as hard as I can to turn up as a slim person.

Just prior to one of these reunions, I had been having a particularly stressful time at work. I had just started my first job in hospitality as human resources manager on an island in the Whitsundays. We knew no-one on the island, the CEO was not supportive of my new role and his managers reflected this lack of interest or commitment to the HR measures that needed to be implemented. Add to that the generous restaurant discounts for senior staff, and I was having to wear the men's version of the island's staff uniform.

As soon as we landed in Melbourne, I had to find a plus-size clothes store prior to attending any of the social activities. I stood in the changing room of that Maggie T shop, staring at my over-fleshed reflection in the mirror. I burst into tears. I was forty-two-years old, and my self-loathing was at an all-time high.

Looking back, I realise that I was once again feeling unsafe and threatened in an environment over which I had no control. Whenever I felt this way, I would turn to food as my solace. Lots and lots of food.

And then I would become the Michelin man.

That image had been with me for many years. Whenever I thought about how I had developed a 'spare tyre,' he would appear. Surrounded in tyres, a pleasant cheery fellow who seemed very happy to be covered in excess weight. I would see myself in that image. I was not happy that I had again gained weight, but I would adopt the cheerful disposition as though it were a character in one of my childhood plays. Another role, another act.

I returned from Melbourne, and like an alcoholic, it was time to rejoin my equivalent of Alcoholics Anonymous. Weight Watchers.

I was living on an island, so I tried the online version of their programme.

For a time, I was able to stick to their points programme and lose enough weight for others to notice.

During my successful weight loss periods, I could enjoy several months of being thin. Well, thinner. I would never achieve *thin*. But I could usually diet from whatever my starting weight. I was buying size 22 at Maggie T, and finish up as a size 10.

Oh, how I love shopping for size-10 clothes instead of size 'tent.' The shopping world is so much more expansive when you are able to fit into a size 10. You can go into any clothes shop and find your size on the rack, on the shelf. And it is so much better if you are able to stay in that slimmer range because as soon as your weight starts to increase, the larger size clothes become harder and harder to find—as evidenced by my typical encounter with the size-8 salesperson

I approached her as she rehung and rearranged clothes on the racks.

'I am wondering if you have these jeans in a size 18?'

'No, we have sold out of them. Come to think of it, we always seem to sell out of the 16s and 18s first.'

I am sure that my silent scream reverberated around the world. But I remained the epitome of calm.

'Could you suggest to your manager that she order more of those larger sizes, given that you sell out so quickly?'

She smiled weakly and rushed off to help a customer who had a greater likelihood of actually fitting into their clothes.

I had to find the 'tent' shops which accommodate

the fuller figure, the 'Woman' styles, the 'Big and Tall.' To add insult to the injury of being overweight and thoroughly displeased with my increased proportions, these shops charge a great deal more for their products. I suppose it's all those extra yards of material.

One of the major differences between people who are size 10 and people who are size 'tent,' is how their clothes fit into a suitcase. I spent a weekend with a friend who was in the former category at a time when I was well and truly in the thick of the latter. She had a small overnight bag from which she was able to produce a vast array of different outfits. Tiny skinny jeans, wispy camisole tops with shoestring straps, petite blouses, cropped t-shirts and shorts, a bikini— even cardigans that were streamlined and non-chunky.

And what about her undies? On size-10 people, you can go to specialty shops where you buy glamorous items they call lingerie. Even the word sounds light and feathery. Bras so small that they disappear into the palm of your hand. Petite G-strings the width of dental floss. An entire week's worth of her lingerie fitted into one cup of my double-D bras.

On size 'tent' people, undergarments are called underwear. Underwear is sensible and comfortable. It comprises full briefs (now there is a misnomer) for those poor souls who can only look at lingerie through beautifully adorned shop windows, as though peering at exotic zoo animals. You are both from different worlds, and you need to stay on your side of the glass.

And of course, the aforementioned gigantic bras are made from several metres of elastane. I think the Germans say it best—bustenhalter. Substantial, serious, with a job to do. Nothing lightweight about that.

All this supersized underclothing takes up a lot of space. Throw in large blouses, wide pants, hefty cardies, a swimsuit with enough surface area to trawl for krill, and my collection of luggage resembled that of a passenger arriving for a first-class cabin on the Titanic.

So often I have turned to humour to cope with my weight issues—to be the 'butt' of my own jokes.

Years later, I was to learn that its cause could be found lurking far below my cuddly exterior, and it was no laughing matter.

27

THE LOST CHILD

'You are surrounded by rings—rings of tyres. Just like the Michelin man. You are encircled—protected—by these rings.'

I was spending time at my favourite health retreat. This was not my first visit to this extraordinary woman with the ability to see into my soul—and to find ways of healing it.

And she was using the image of the Michelin man. How could she know that I had often used that image to describe myself?

On this occasion, the topic of our session was my weight and my constant, lifelong struggle with dieting. I was frustrated by my lack of success, which I believed was due to my lack of discipline. Surely, all I needed to do was to keep eating *good* food and to limit my intake of *bad* food. Why did I always find that so difficult?

And now my trusted healer was telling me that this Michelin man of tyres was there to protect my body.

'Why do you think my body needs protection? From

what?' I was fifty-seven-years old. I was quite capable of looking after myself.

'It is your inner child. The little girl who felt so unsafe, all those years ago. She still lives within you. And whenever she feels unsafe, she puts on those tyres as a shield.'

I thought, *That child must have felt unsafe for most of my life, given the number of years I have surrounded her with those rubber spheres.*

I said, 'So what can I do about that? How do I make her feel safe, let her know that she is no longer in danger?'

'You need to speak to this child. You need to remind her how special and wonderful she is. Tell her she is loved and valued. And most importantly, let her know that she has nothing to feel ashamed or guilty about. None of what happened to her was ever her fault. She didn't deserve to be treated badly.'

I had no idea that my inner child could still be feeling the pain of all those years past. But as the therapist spoke, I could feel the truth of what she was saying.

I had built a wall around myself as an attempt to protect the child from harm. It was a sheath of rubber, which acted as an insulator from hurt and pain—an impenetrable wall of neoprene.

By now, the tears were flowing.

She went on. 'She was just in the wrong place and had no means of escape. But she is free at last. Tell her how proud you are of her. Let her know that you are sorry for not being aware of her pain and needs in the past, and for pushing her too hard sometimes to try and impress others. Tell her that you will be her guardian and protector from now on. Everything will be okay, and you will never let her come to any more harm. You will always be there for her.'

My tears turned to wracking sobs—so guttural that they caused my whole body to heave and shake. It was as though I was trying to spew forth the decades of hidden hurt and secret shame, purging it from my body.

The terrified child was being released, and my broken soul was seeking to be cleansed and reborn.

I slumped in the armchair, exhausted by this primordial howling and surprised by a new sensation of lightness and an encircling calm.

She closed her eyes and took a long deep breath. It was as though we had been in a séance, and she had been channelling the spirit of my long-buried child.

She reopened her eyes and took my hands in hers.

'How are you feeling?'

'Like I've been hit by a very large truck.'

Her smile was warm and encouraging.

'Your reaction to this session indicates that the child within you had much grieving to do. It might not feel like it right now, but this was a very good start. Now the healing process can begin.'

My time was up—another client was waiting at the door.

I stood up and swayed from side to side. I was exhausted.

'You will feel very tired now. Please go back to your room, lie down and be very very kind to her for the rest of the day.'

We hugged—a long deep hug. I left her warm embrace and navigated my way back to my room.

As I lay on my bed, I was overwhelmed by a new truth.

While I was certainly going to be kind to that child for the rest of the day, I now knew that I needed to be kind to her, and to myself, for the rest of our lives.

ACT 4
THE FINAL CURTAIN

A NEW COURAGE

My father sighed in his sleep. During this visit, he had certainly slept for much longer periods than he had been awake.

I was once again drawn to the shelf and one photo in particular. This was one of my brother Mark and my father, which took me back to the day it was taken, eighteen years earlier. My father's hair was windblown, and he had a wry, proud look on his face. Mark was smiling, as big as I had ever seen, on his wedding day. His arm was around my father's shoulders, and he looked the picture of happiness. The church formalities had been concluded, and we were off to the reception.

This was the latest in a series of family events over the years—the first birthday of a nephew in 1990, my mother's sixtieth birthday in 1993, Jeffrey's wedding in 1995, a family reunion at the Windsor Hotel in Melbourne, celebrating the thirtieth anniversary of our arrival in Australia in 1996, and that same year, my sister's wedding on board a cruiser on the Yarra

River—where the whole family got together to celebrate even after everyone knew what my father had done. This was the third wedding we were celebrating where unknowing family and guests would continue to believe that we were a normal, functioning family. It was as though those revelations from twelve years earlier had taken place in a parallel universe which had no effect on our current existence.

In the months preceding this celebration, I had made a huge decision that I knew would have far reaching implications for my whole family. I had decided this would be the last time I would continue to live the charade, the façade, of pretending that being in my father's presence was fine and the dreadful events of those previous years were somehow erased. I felt as if it was not as though he had been given a clean slate—it was as if his slate had never been sullied.

For me, this living lie had become more and more untenable. I felt nauseous around him, unsafe and threatened. I was thirty-nine-years-old and knew that I was now physically safe, but his presence awakened the frightened seven-year-old, and it was time her voice was heard. This game of 'Happy Families' had been played for too long, and like the poker game that ran non-stop for eight years at the Bird Cage Hotel in Tombstone, Arizona, players were getting very tired, and the game no longer held the same appeal.

For months, I had been contemplating my need to deal with those years of bottled-up feelings and bring them out in the open.

It was very wrong that he had lived a life unchanged by those past events, either those of my childhood or the revelations of 1986. For him, there had been no consequences—not a single one.

I had never taken the path of formal, judicial punishment. The police had no knowledge of his criminal behavior, he had never been charged with a felony and he had spent no time in jail.

He was seventy-seven-years-old, and as far as I was concerned, it was time that he suffered some consequences for his appalling actions. It was time—past time—that he got a meaningful punishment.

Finally, I knew what I needed to do.

I was the warden who could administer the cruelest punishment of all.

The events of that weekend might have unfolded quite differently.

In spite of the revelations of 1986 and the dozen years that had passed since, my mother chose to stay with my father.

When I questioned her decision, she said, 'Forty years ago, we married for better or worse, and I guess it doesn't get much worse than this.'

This statement seemed so naïve in the face of all that had happened, but I realised that my mother's upbringing must have shaped her view of the world and in particular, her relationship with my father.

She was a child of the Second World War, with a father who was absent in France and India for a period of six years. She had been six-years-old when he left for war and almost a teenager when he returned, an idealised war hero of the family. His uniformed photo was kept on the mantelpiece. His heroic status reinforced by my grandmother and society at large.

She has always described his homecoming as strange. He had been gone for such a long time, especially in a child's eyes. 'We didn't really know him, and it was different, having a man in the house.'

He returned to his pre-war job as a sales representative for a clothing company, which also entailed him being away from home on a regular basis.

Both her father and her husband were veterans of that war. I have wondered whether she idealised my father as she had done with her own father. With veterans as the only male role models in her life, perhaps she regarded them all as war heroes. Unconsciously holding my father up as a hero likely meant she expected he would be a good father, as her father had been to her. It certainly allowed her to forgive my father for his crimes.

She once confided that she had often told her friends, with great pride, about how close I was with my father, and that she had regarded our close relationship as a positive sign of a healthy connection between us. I've come to wonder whether this miscalculation was the result of the absence of a relationship with her own father. She had no role model of a loving, present father, and so likely did not suspect my father's interest in me was anything but normal. In fact, in her mind, it probably made up for everything she had been denied in her own childhood. This may explain my mother's lack of awareness regarding the danger I was in.

I believe that being married mattered a great deal to her. Her identity was very much shaped as his wife and our mother, so she chose to stay with him at any cost. Later, she did leave him. But even after their separation, she would still remember their wedding anniversary each year and pronounce the number of years since their wedding day, as though they were still together. Despite their separation, they never formalised it with a divorce.

Most of her friends did not know the reason for the separation. I imagine they presumed that they had drifted apart, given the thirteen-year age difference.

After she knew of the abuse, she still continued to talk about him as the love of her life. She appreciated and admired what a good provider he was, the way he cared for his family, including the support he gave her parents financially when they emigrated to Australia as well as his long-widowed mother and eldest brother. She was able to compartmentalise these qualities of dependability and generosity from his other monstrous side.

I genuinely believe my mother did not know about the abuse. But equally, I believe she *should* have known. As a child, I should have been able to go to my mother when the abuse began. Or at least in subsequent years. Whatever the dynamics of our dysfunctional family, I never blamed her or held her responsible. I blamed myself, for being The Secret keeper. The keeping of The Secret had been so instilled in me that I wore it as a badge of honour for over twenty years—my invisible Victoria Cross awarded for valour in the face of the enemy.

Though I have never accused her, she has held herself responsible. She said, 'I only really ever had one job, and that was to keep you children safe. And I failed at it. I failed to keep you safe. That will be a lifelong regret.'

I have forgiven my mother for the sins of omission, for not being more vigilant, more suspicious of my 'wonderfully close' relationship with my father.

I've never uttered the words to her but rather displayed my forgiveness in continuing to maintain a relationship with her in the years since the revelation.

But in the months leading up to Mark's wedding, I told her that her choice was becoming untenable for me. While she and dad were living under the same roof, the situation was unworkable. My tolerance was now at breaking point.

'Mum, the time has come for you to decide where you stand and whose corner you're in. I feel that you have chosen sides, and from my point of view, you have very much chosen the wrong side. I will not be able to continue to see you if you stay with him.'

I knew I was giving her an ultimatum, but I was clear in my decision. It was either him or me.

My words had their desired effect. A few weeks after this conversation, she told me that she was going to leave my father; and now that she had made the decision, she was going to make this happen as soon as possible.

I was gratified that my words had elicited this outcome but appalled at her timing.

It was less than a fortnight to Mark's wedding.

'Mum, listen. Given that this decision has been so long in coming, and we have a family wedding taking place very shortly, you are going to have to keep this to yourself. If I can suck it up and get through this family event, then so can you. There is to be nothing that spoils Mark's big day.'

I was crystal clear about this. As the lead actor, producer and director of this game of family charades, I felt that I had more entitlement than others to determine how it should be played.

I think she was surprised that I wasn't more supportive of her decision and its immediate implementation. But she agreed that she would say nothing to my father or the rest of the family until after the wedding.

I was driven by the knowledge that I had made a significant decision about my relationship with my father, and I did not want anyone or anything to take away from the timing and effect of my carefully conceived plans.

I had definitely earned that right.

The wedding proceeded with all the outward appearances of an intact family.

For one last time.

I stared down at the expunged contents of my stomach as they were flushed into the bowels of the porcelain bowl. *So that is what an expensive wedding feast looks like twelve hours after the event*, I thought.

I wiped my lips and stared at myself in the mirror. I reapplied my lipstick, straightened my blouse and rejoined the crowd.

Yesterday, the ballroom had been filled with incredulous gasps, laughter and tears as Harry Connick Junior's 'It Had to Be You' was played and our newlyweds, after adopting the perfect pose, performed a flawless waltz across the floor. No awkward bridal shuffle for this pair. They had been taking dance lessons in order to produce this surprise gift to us all.

It was the day after the wedding. The weekend was culminating with a lunchtime barbeque in the beer garden of a Brisbane hotel. All the guests and relatives who had stayed overnight in town were invited, and there was lots of food, alcohol and laughter. Everyone was having a wonderful time.

Except me.

I knew that this was the day that my father's consequence-free existence would come to an end. I had been rehearsing the words I would say to him for weeks, but having those words travel from my head to his ears would be a journey far more challenging than the short distance would suggest. I continued to circle the courtyard, chatting with others and giving the outward appearance of a sister who was happy for her little brother. And I was. But all the while, the rat I was about to release gnawed at my innards, making my palms clammy.

The event was winding down and a few guests

began to leave, saying their farewells to the bride and groom. Soon I would feel too exposed if I took my father to one side for a confidential chat. I felt the safety in the number of people who were still hovering, eating and ordering just one more jug of beer.

The moment was now.

He was standing to one side, observing the crowd and seemed to be in a world of his own thoughts. I came up beside him, summoned all my courage and began to speak.

'I have something very important to say to you, so I need you to give me your full attention and listen very carefully.' I knew that this sounded very formal, but it was all part of the rehearsed speech.

He turned towards me, a quizzical look on his face and that sideways smile that suddenly resembled a leer. Unexpectedly, he took both my hands in his.

I froze. What was he doing? How dare he make such a warm, personal gesture at this time, when I had something to say I knew he would not want to hear? Was he trying to disarm me? Had he some inkling of what lay ahead? But I had mentioned my plan to no-one, not even my husband, so that was not it.

Conscious of the people around, I did not pull my hands away but let them lie, inert, on his palms. It seemed easier, and oddly, I felt calmer with them there. I was so confident of my next move, I was not going to allow anything, any gesture, to get in my way.

'Dad, I can't do this anymore. I can't play the game of pretending that everything is okay between us.'

He continued to hold my hands, a little tighter it seemed.

'There have been no consequences for you. It is as if the events of my childhood, and the revelations of 1986, did not happen. Your life hasn't changed. Not only that, you still have no remorse for what you did. You have never apologised, have never taken any responsibility and I have had enough.'

The words were somersaults, tumbling out of my mouth, and I was speaking more and more quickly. I just had to get through this. I had to get to the end of my speech, which now bore no resemblance to the one I thought I'd prepared.

'So I need you to understand—this will be the last time that I see you. Ever.'

I paused, waiting for his reaction, a comment, any clue that he had grasped the enormity of what I had said.

He squeezed my hands and then let them fall.

He breathed heavily. 'I thought that everything was okay between you and me. That enough time had passed. You have never said or done anything to make me think otherwise.'

I was stunned as he tossed my well-rehearsed speech into a sea of my disbelief.

Was it my responsibility to tell him that his behavior had been wrong? Had he no insights into the crime he had committed? Did he truly believe that because I had said nothing, everything was okay between us?

In that moment, I became aware that he was forcing the child within me to accept the blame for his actions. In his mind, this was all my fault.

And worse, he was suggesting that the wound he'd

inflicted must surely be healed because so much time had passed.

Once again, my silence had served me poorly.

'No, Dad. Everything is not okay. It has not been since I was a child. It has never been okay between us, but for the sake of appearances, I have continued to pretend that nothing is wrong. It has always been wrong, and now I am finally telling you. I will not see you again. Not only that, I will be telling the rest of the family that they are not to tell you anything about what is happening in my life. I am cutting myself off from you entirely and forever.'

And with that, I delivered my knock-out blow. After months of searching for the most suitable penalty, I knew this was the most severe form of punishment I could administer.

My world had always been his world. I had continued to allow him access to every aspect of my adult life. He basked in the reflected glory of my successes. I knew how proud he was of my achievements and how I had lived an extraordinary life.

And now it would be lost to him—forever.

There was only one more thing to say.

'Goodbye, Dad.'

And so it was done. After all that had passed, after the years of charades and burying my feelings about the abuse, this was the culmination of a lifetime of hurt and betrayal. In those two simple words, I felt that I had taken the bravest stand of all. He would be out of my life, at last.

I turned and walked briskly towards the exit. The tears flowed down my cheeks. I needed to get out of there before anyone saw me. I could apologise later for the lack of cordial farewells.

Finally, I had done the right thing for me. The years of lies, pretense, game playing, were over. I had taken back my life, my sense of self-worth, my honour, my integrity—I had taken back *me*.

But what I did not count on was an unexpected, complicated, confusing and illogical emotion which overlayed all these feelings. I was distraught at the loss of my father, at the ending of our relationship. Surely, that made no sense.

Of course, with time, I have come to understand that what I was grieving was the loss of the idea of my father, the myth. Whilst we had remained in contact in a world of make-believe, the myth remained alive. We had played our parts in a 'normal' parent-and-child relationship, behaving as normal fathers and daughters were meant to behave. We had each perfected our roles. As they say at the start of a play, when there has been a change to the advertised players, 'The parts of the father and daughter will be played by…'

Beneath the roles, a different reality had always lurked. And now that I'd torn down the masks, the show was over for good.

I walked along the Brisbane streets, letting my tears dry in the mild April air. I felt as though my body was self-propelled, as though floating above the footpath. Was I really lighter than air? Is this what it felt like to be emancipated? After decades of being a slave to my own sense of duty, societal norms and my lack of courage, I had taken this final stand. The shackles of my past—the shackles that should have been my father's to wear—were loosening from my limbs.

I had begun the day as Harmonia, the goddess of harmony and concord. For too long I had lived under the spell of my father, subservient to him in every way. But now I had emerged free from his bonds, as Athena from the forehead of her father Zeus. I was all powerful, clad in my battle armor. I had used my wisdom, courage and warrior skills to administer law and justice.

I think the goddesses would have been proud.

THE LETTER (PART 2)

October 2015
I sat in the back pew of that Catholic church, reading the long-awaited letter and catching my cascading tears in already sodden tissues. I was not alone. I was joined by a shadow cast of former selves, each of whom deserved to be there. We had all waited so long to know the letter's content.

The seven-year-old, frightened and confused by the visiting Darkness; the nine-year-old, who scurried away from The Chair which had almost ruptured The Secret; the frightened and confused thirteen-year-old, who wondered why sometimes The Dressing Gown abandoned her (Didn't he love her anymore?); the wiser sixteen-year-old who learned she had the power to extinguish The Torch; and the nineteen-year-old who had said, 'Enough.'

But now, sitting in that church was the accomplished, educated, professional woman, who had lived through all these times, determined never to be a victim, and who had chosen to live a life beyond survival. She had chosen to thrive.

As I held the letter in my hands, I pondered the words I had just read—words all my former selves had been waiting a lifetime to hear.

It was an apology. In his unmistakable handwriting, he had said sorry after years of denying that his actions required contrition.

He also took responsibility for his actions, acknowledging that he had betrayed me and had failed in his duty of trust as a parent.

He did not seek or expect forgiveness. He simply wanted me to know his feelings, and he had finally put them in writing.

He admired my successes and told me I was a special lady.

He wished me future happiness.

He signed off 'Your genuinely remorseful father.'

It was overwhelming to finally receive this unexpected apology in writing while he was still alive. I cried, without understanding what my tears signified.

I felt the lifting of a lifetime's burden that had sat so heavily on my shoulders and chest, casting its shadow over my heart and smothering my soul under a blanket of shame and guilt. At long last, he had taken responsibility for his actions, acknowledging he had betrayed my trust as his child.

I fixated on the words, 'genuinely remorseful.' Never once had he displayed regret or uttered these words to me; and now, here they were in writing, a permanent record of his wrongdoing, of his guilt. Now said, they could not be unsaid.

He was not seeking or expecting forgiveness. He

recognised that his actions were of such magnitude that they could not be forgiven.

It was his acceptance that forgiveness was not expected or warranted, which made my realisation all the more profound.

I had always known he was fallible, a man physically and emotionally broken by war and his own lifetime of imperfections. As I sat catching my tears, I knew that long ago, in my heart, I had already forgiven him.

It took much longer to forgive myself because I had held myself responsible for his actions. I had not discouraged his unwanted and unnatural attentions, so I had always felt I was in some way to blame for the abuse. Whilst I acknowledged superficially that the guilt and blame lay with him, subconsciously, I had continued to blame myself well into adulthood.

I'd been besieged by doubts. Surely, I could have made him stop, should have made him stop, especially as I got older? Not only that, perhaps there was something wrong with me because at times, I waited for his nightly appearance and felt rejected if he did not visit. I had grown to look forward to the illicit sex, found that I enjoyed the pleasurable sensations, and enjoyed giving him the pleasure that seemed so evident during our encounters. And because the relationship had been based on love, always on love, I had never stopped loving him. As a daughter should love her father.

I may have hated his actions, but I had never hated the man. He was my father. Had always been my father, and that love had run so strong and so deep.

I gathered up the letter and headed out of the church. I knew what I needed to do next.

EXIT, STAGE RIGHT

The room was darkening as the last rays of the afternoon sun disappeared beneath the venetian blinds.

'I have to go, Dad. I have to drive to Melbourne and then I have to catch a plane.' It occurred to me that although we had spent the whole day together, he still did not know where I lived. I had not told him, and he hadn't asked. But it did not matter—all that mattered to both of us was that I had come to visit him.

He stirred and refocussed his cloudy eyes.

Once again, he struggled to speak the words. Eventually, he said, 'Your visit has been… invaluable.'

'You think my visit has been invaluable?'

'Yes. There is nothing to replace it. It has been very special indeed.'

He paused, his face contorted, as though struggling to find his next words.

'You know, I have always loved you.'

'Yes, Dad. I know—I have always known that you loved me.'

I knew what I would say next. Had known since I had made the decision to travel over two thousand kilometres to see my father.

'And I have always loved you, Dad.'

In spite of everything that had happened, I knew this to be true.

He seemed surprised by my words.

'Well, there is no logic in that, is there?'

'No, you are right. There is no logic in that. But you were my father... are still my father...' My words faltered as the tears streamed down my cheeks.

'Dad, do you know why I have come here today? I've come to tell you something very important.'

As he struggled to focus on my words, on my face, I wondered if I had left my visit too long—that he was past the point of being able to understand why I had come. *Please don't let this be for nothing. All the soul searching—it has to mean something. For both of us. He has to be able to understand. He has to know that I have come so far—and not just in distance.*

He had already told me that he did not seek or expect forgiveness.

But those words made my decision even more important.

In the months since I had read his letter, I had been consumed by the idea of forgiveness. What did it mean to forgive someone? What is true forgiveness? Why was this so important to me? Would it be important to him?

As I had reclaimed my power on that day eighteen years earlier, this choice to forgive was completely within my control.

Christians believe that the act of forgiveness is to let go of the transgression. They do not condone the act or behave as though it did not happen. They also believe that a person can only be forgiven if they are truly repentant of their wrongdoing, of their sin. When we forgive others, we are then able to receive forgiveness from God, for our own sins.

The Lord's Prayer invokes us to 'forgive us our trespasses as we forgive those who trespass against us.'

I had said these words over and over since I was a young child, and yet I had never really understood their true meaning until that moment.

I needed to forgive my own trespasses, because even though they were not mine, I had believed them to be and had carried them around as a lifelong burden.

I took my father's shrivelled hand in mine and said the words that I needed him to hear.

'I want you to know... I have come... I have come to tell you that I forgive you, Dad. You are forgiven.'

These three words were to be a pronouncement of biblical proportions, as though I was some divine, forgiving messenger. Instead, they were lost as they struggled to leave my tear-swollen throat.

I formed my fingers into fists and pressed them into my thighs as I sucked air deep into my lungs. This was the whole purpose of my visit. I was not some casual caller who had popped in for idle conversation or to feed him spoonfuls of lunch. He needed to know that this moment was extraordinary—he needed to appreciate the enormity of this trek.

'I forgive you, Dad.'

He turned towards me, his piercing eyes staring deep into mine. I could see my tears mirrored in his.

His eyes closed, and he laid his head back on the pillow. He sighed deeply, then said, more clearly than he had spoken all day, 'Now I can die in peace.'

I took his hands in mine.

'Please tell me that you haven't been waiting for this, waiting for me to come, so that you could...' I grappled for the word, '...go?'

'Not waiting,' he paused,' but... hoping.'

The box of tissues beside his bed was now empty. I wiped my dripping nose on my sleeve and scrabbled through my bag, searching for the packet that I knew was there.

How long had he been hoping?

If I had not come, had not said the words, would he have died a tormented death?

In spite of our past, in spite of the childhood that he had taken, I did not want this to be his end.

It confirmed the rightness of my decision.

Although he did not seek or expect forgiveness, it mattered. Being forgiven mattered. For me and for him.

To see him at peace, knowing that it had been in my power to give him that peace, I felt generous and kind. Uplifted.

The punishment—the one that had been on my choosing—had served its purpose. He had been in the wilderness of my life for eighteen years, and he had done his time.

His warden had granted him pardon. He was free to go.

And so was I.

Free to go on with the rest of my life. Free from the spectre of the past that had continued to fill the unseen parts of my world.

I scooped up the pile of sodden tissues and dropped them in the bin. The crying was over.

I gathered up my belongings and stood, looking down on his ever-diminishing figure, still swaddled in that non-descript blanket.

'I'll come and see you again soon, Dad. We'll be in Victoria in a few weeks, and I'll come and see you then. Will that be okay?' His eyes filled with tears, and he managed to nod.

I wanted to leave him with the hope that the relationship had been rekindled.

But even as I said those words, I knew that I would never see him again. I believe that he knew it too.

It was not because his frailty meant that every day, the staff were surprised by his waking. It was not because his life now hung by the lightest of gossamer threads.

It was because there was nothing more to say.

It had all been said.

So now it was time to leave.

I kissed him on his forehead and stroked his hair.

'Bye, Dad.'

I walked out of the home and into the cool of the late afternoon.

My heart felt a new lightness, and a warm glow filled the spaces of my widening soul.

Indira Gandhi said, 'Forgiveness is a virtue of the brave.'

I had never felt more brave, wise or complete.
Athena still lived strong in me, but today, she had been joined by Clementia.
And forgiveness, mercy and absolution walked with me.
In that moment, I found a new certainty.
You can forgive the unforgiveable.

POSTSCRIPT

A Funeral

As Leonard Cohen sang 'Hallelujah,' the service began. The celebrant welcomed those gathered and read from Ecclesiastes.

'To everything there is a season and a time for every purpose under heaven. A time to be born, a time to die… a time to love, a time to hate.'

Speeches were made, recalling the deceased's early days. They told the story of how he joined the military so that he could be a part of the adventure that besieged the world in 1939. Stories of how he had survived the most terrible of experiences during that war and how he had made a life in Australia for his family. A true phoenix rising from the ashes of a lost generation.

The grandchildren took it in turns to recount their memories of their grandfather. Remembering a man who brought laughter and love into their homes, who was kind and supportive, and who adored his grandchildren.

The final gesture was given by a member of the local RSL, who read aloud his service history. Each of the assembled was invited to lay a poppy on the flag-covered casket, a further recognition of his life not only as a father, grandfather and friend, but as a man who had served his country.

It was all so proper, fitting and 'normal'—precisely how a person who had lived into his nineties should be remembered.

But as I placed my poppy among the pile, my tears were not for the deceased in the casket.

I had never met this man. He was a complete stranger to me. I had gone to support my husband as he honoured the passing of a friend. A returned POW from the Second World War, John had sat with him on many occasions at his retirement village, listening to his stories from the past and marvelling at the bravery of this old soldier.

My tears were for the father I had loved and had forgiven, and for whom I was still grieving.

He had died only weeks after my visit. The ravages of age and ailments had taken their toll, and he was gone.

Jeffrey had rung each of us the following morning to tell us of his passing, which had occurred the night before.

'I'm sorry for your loss,' he said.

Why did he speak like a detective from an American crime show? 'It is your loss too,' I'd said. 'We have both lost our father.'

I began to cry before the call was over.

Jeffrey took care of the funeral arrangements and was the sole mourner. It was as though this was the final phase in his duty of care to my father, and he neither encouraged nor sought any support on that day.

For my father, it had been an unadorned coffin—no flowers, no flag, no poppies. The eulogy, which he had written for himself, was read to an echoing chapel. There were no speeches, no recognition of his military service or to the sacrifice that he had made for his country of birth, no celebration of a life that never fully recovered from those deep, unseen scars. He was an imperfect man—physically harmed by the trauma of war and emotionally inept.

In accordance with his final instructions, and completely consistent with his love of this composer, Beethoven's Symphony No. 7 had been played. Not the entire symphony but as he had specifically and explicitly chosen, just the fourth movement.

At the same time, as the music swelled in that far distant church, I too was listening to its powerful and stirring strains. My mother and sister were in their own homes, doing the same.

I had selected a YouTube performance of the piece by the Israel Philharmonic Orchestra—a nod to his Jewish heritage. John squeezed my hand as I pressed 'play' on my mobile phone.

I wept for the entire seven minutes. Not tears for the man who had passed but tears for the man he could have been, that he should have been and for our relationship that never had a chance to be 'normal.' Tears for the child whose innocence was lost so long ago.

I sat in our courtyard, listening to the strains of that powerful piece of music. I felt the cooling shadows of the tall grass trees in their glistening blue pots and smelled the gentle fragrance of the jasmine flowers wafting through the stillness of the afternoon.

I pondered those words, 'a time to love, a time to hate.'

For me, in spite of all that I had endured, I knew that I had chosen love over hate and that knowledge brought me a new peace.

As I walked back into the house, I felt the lifting of a heaviness that had pervaded my life for so many years. He had now succumbed to that most final of judgements, and I had shed my tears over him for the very last time.

ACKNOWLEDGEMENTS

This book would not have been 'birthed' without the unwavering and unconditional support of Joanne Fedler.

From the moment we met at the Golden Door in 2016, she was committed to supporting me to write my story. At all times, I felt validated and held in her extraordinarily capable hands and generous and caring heart. The relationship that developed between us is so much more than mentor and author—it is one of mutual respect. Her depth of understanding about what a writer needs to pen a memoir, and the patience and space she gave me to be the best version of my writing self has given rise to a friendship that I will always value and treasure.

In May of that same year, I met my writing 'tribe' on her writing retreat in Fiji—what a privilege it was to spend time with this group of talented and amazing women. I have so appreciated their support over the years. Later, this tribe expanded to include our Silver and Gold Wings writing buddies—your explicit and implicit support has been with me throughout my writing process.

I want to thank Norie Libradilla for her final proofread and for ensuring the manuscript had been thoroughly detailed.

To Carol George for her manuscript assessment which gave me such useful feedback and to Alison Arnold for her structural review—the day we spent together was invaluable and reassured me that my writing would be worth reading.

I want to make special mention of:

Kylie, who read the early draft of my book and gave such honest and helpful feedback, as well as for being a true friend throughout these years.

Pip, who accompanied me on our three writing retreats, all of which helped to progress and improve the telling of my story.

Lisa, who is always there to support her writing friends in whatever capacity is needed—selflessly and enthusiastically.

Lorraine, who was there for me on 'that' day. We had only known each other for a few months but she sensed exactly what I needed and gave it in spades. Your kindness will never be forgotten.

To John, my husband and number one fan. Your love and support has never wavered in over forty years and I am grateful for you every single day.

And to my sister. You accept me without judgement, you fill my life with joy, courage and grace and I feel that I am a better person with you in my life.

ABOUT THE AUTHOR

Louise Ryan was born to the sound of the York Minster bells in 1958 and can trace her lineage back to William the Conqueror. She was emigrated to Australia by her parents in 1967. As 'Ten Pound Poms,' they voyaged through the Mediterranean and Suez Canal, landing in Melbourne on St. Patrick's Day. As a young child, she thought that all new arrivals were greeted by hordes of people dressed in green and waving shamrocks. A studious child who loved to sing and act, she found the world of make-believe to be a safe and magical place.

After finishing school, she auditioned for NIDA and is still waiting for them to call back.

Instead, she had a successful career in the world of human resources. Recently, the universe used drastic measures to gain her attention and she decided that there were more important things in life than climbing the corporate ladder.

Louise lives on the Sunshine Coast of Australia with her husband John.

www.ingramcontent.com/pod-product-compliance
Lightning Source LLC
Chambersburg PA
CBHW042045280426
43661CB00094B/1017